-0. NOV. 1983

D1433358

BOKONYI, S.
Przevalsky horse 74 16999
599·665

Please renew/return this item by the last date shown.

So that your telephone call is charged at local rate, please call the numbers as set out below:

|  | From Area codes 01923 or 0208: | From the rest of Herts: |
|---|---|---|
| Renewals: | 01923 471373 | 01438 737373 |
| Enquiries: | 01923 471333 | 01438 737333 |
| Minicom: | 01923 471599 | 01438 737599 |

L32b

**Hertfordshire**
COUNTY COUNCIL

Community Information

02|07

1 3 NOV 2008

9/12

L32a

# THE PRZEVALSKY HORSE

# THE PRZEVALSKY
# HORSE

DR. SÁNDOR BÖKÖNYI

Translated from the Hungarian
by
LILI HALÁPY

SOUVENIR PRESS

WATFORD CENTRAL

Copyright © 1974 by Dr Sándor Bökönyi
English translation Copyright © 1974 by Souvenir Press Ltd
All rights reserved

First published 1974 by Souvenir Press Ltd,
95 Mortimer Street, London W1N 8HP
and simultaneously in Canada by
J. M. Dent & Sons (Canada) Ltd,
Ontario, Canada

No part may be reproduced in any form without permission in
writing from the publisher except by a reviewer who wishes to
quote brief passages for the purposes of a review.

ISBN 0 285 62110 6

HERTFORDSHIRE
COUNTY LIBRARY
599·725
74 16999
17. JAN. 1975

Printed in Great Britain by
Clarke, Doble & Brendon Ltd,
Plymouth

# CONTENTS

# LIST OF ILLUSTRATIONS

*Between pages 64 and 65*

7

decessors, considering the period and the geographic situation.

6 Homotype of the Mongolian wild horse (in profile) in the Zoological Institute of the Soviet Academy of Sciences in Leningrad. Collected by Colonel Przevalsky.

7 The same, seen from the front.

8 The same, seen from the back.

9 Drawing of a Mongolian wild horse in Przevalsky's book. It was probably made by I. V. Roborovsky, a member of Przevalsky's expedition, who later continued the Colonel's exploratory work. Though the drawing presents numerous characteristic features of the Mongolian wild horse it delineates the legs in a way similar to those of noble domestic ones: exaggerating the shortness of the dockhairs, it shows the tail almost as if it were that of an ass.

10 Hamlet, Budapest Zoo, May 1970. On account of the long winter the shedding of hairs was protracted and the mane grew too long. The horizontal stripes above the hocks of the forelegs are clearly discernible.

11 Hamlet, showing the massive neck and the whitish colour around the mouth. The mane, grown too long because of the long winter, hangs to the forehead.

12 Hamlet.

13 Hamlet. The hairs on the dock are short, and the dorsal stripe extends to the tail. Photo Konya.

14 Horizontal stripes on the forelegs of the six-year-old Mongolian wild stallion Hamlet. Photo Konya.

15 16 & 17 Skull of Przevalsky stallion. Martin Duther Universität, Julius Kühn Collection, Halle/Saale. Photo Londner.

18 Mongolian wild horses playing at Askania Nova. Photo Anghi.

19 Wild horse. Incised decoration of a Tartar wooden bucket from the Altai. After Ivanov.

20 Tarpan. From the mural of the Sophia Church in Kiev. After Heptner.

21 Mongolian domestic horse, whose skull is strongly reminiscent of Mongolian wild horses, with silver studded bridle and saddle. Photo Erdélyi.

22 Mongolian horsemen, one of them with a lasso with stick. Photo Teichert.

23 The dorsal and lumbar vertebrae, grown together, of the horse from the Avar tomb at Keszthely. In profile. Photo Karát.

24 The same seen from below..

25 Part of the jaw of the horse from the Avar tomb at Keszthely. Beside the third left incisor and in front of the canine tooth a supernumerary tooth is clearly visible. Photo Karát.

26 Przevalsky foal that died soon after its arrival, from the second Hagenbeck consignment. Naturkunde Museum, Stuttgart.

27 Orlitza III-Mongol, the only Przevalsky mare born in the wild and living in Europe, with her two foals in Askania Nova. Photo Anghi.

28 Group of Mongolian wild horses in Askania Nova. Photo Anghi.

29 Mongolian wild horses in their winter coat in the animal park of Hellabrunn. The long, shaggy hair and the

"beard" below the chin can be clearly observed. Photo Angermayer.

30 Sars (Askania III), a stallion, one of the sons of Orlitza III-Mongol, in his winter coat in Prague Zoo in December 1968. Photo J. Volf.

31 Verita (Praha 79), the Przevalsky mare born in July 1966 in Prague Zoo and transferred to Aalborg in 1969. Photo J. Volf, December 1968.

32 Przevalsky foal in Prague Zoo. Photo J. Volf.

33 Przevalsky stallion in San Diego Zoo, a characteristic example of the light colour variant. The upper third of its tail is covered with short hairs only. The white colouring around the muzzle can also be seen. Photo Bökönyi.

34 Mongolian wild stallion born in free nature, then kept in Talbolug, Mongolia, where it died about 1959. Several hybrids that he sired with Mongolian domestic mares are still alive. Probably this was the wild horse Dr. C. Purkyne mentioned. Photo Tshevegmid.

35 Przevalsky mares at Shargantului, on the model farm for educational purposes at the Academy of Agriculture of Ulan Bator. Both of them were born in the wild and brought to the model farm in 1944. Their further fate is unknown. Photo Purkyne, after Mohr.

36 Mongolia, with the present probable distribution area (hatched part) of the Przevalsky horse.

37 The Takhin Shara-nuru Mountains, the last area to which Mongolian wild horses have withdrawn. Photo Kaszab.

38 Characteristic habitat of the Mongolian wild horse in the Takhin Shara-nuru Mountains. Photo Kaszab.

# PREFACE

The Mongolian wild horse, named, in honour of the late Colonel N. M. Przevalsky (1839—88), the eminent Russian explorer who discovered it, *Equus przewalskii*, is a precious rarity of nature. It is a veritable mystery how such a big, wild mammal could have remained so long unknown to European zoologists. Perhaps because—in much diminished numbers—it fled from man, who threatened its very existence, to one of the parts of Central Asia most difficult of access. Or perhaps because it was confused with its relative, the kulan, the Asian wild ass, which is much more frequently met. Or perhaps because the horse, one of our best-known domestic animals, was not considered an exotic species, so for a long time its wild form did not attract attention.

Who knows? Perhaps its neglect was due to all three reasons, or to even more. Anyhow, Colonel Przevalsky found this wild horse at the most fortunate moment : at a time when Darwin and the Swiss Rütimeyer were drawing zoologists' and breeders' attention to the wild ancestors of domestic animals. Thus when Poliakov publicized the discovery of the Mongolian horse in 1881, on the evidence of the skull and fell Przevalsky had brought back from his second travel in Central Asia in 1878, there

11

was much excitement among scholars at the news. There were of course some who did not consider it an original wild horse but a feral domestic one, others who deemed it to be a half-ass, again others a form between horse and ass. But the overwhelming majority agreed with Poliakov that the Asiatic wild horse had been found.

Soon expeditions set out to study the Mongolian wild horse in its habitat, and to find more material about it for museums. In the last years of the nineteenth century both the Russians and the British hit upon the idea of capturing Przevalsky horses alive and transferring them to Europe for zoos and animal parks. This was soon done and the general public also became acquainted with the newly discovered Mongolian wild horse.

Then the breeding of wild horses in zoos was tried and proved to be successful. Experiments at cross-breeding domestic horses with wild ones, and wild horses with zebras were also successes. And since in the wild Mongolian horses were becoming rarer and rarer—at one time they seemed to be completely extinct—the strange situation emerged that there were more wild horses alive in zoos than in their natural habitat. There have of course been other species of wild animals in this paradoxical situation.

On the other hand, it is rather strange that, although the discovery of the Przevalsky horse created a sensation, and was much discussed, relatively little was written about it. Short articles appeared, but most of these dealt with one or two specialist aspects of the case. The papers presented at two symposia on the Przevalsky horse, held in Prague in 1959 and Berlin in 1965, were published in two volumes (*Equus I*, Prague, 1961; *Equus II*, Berlin, 1967) and a Stud Book of Mongolian wild horses (*General Pedigree Book of the Przevalsky Horse*; Prague, 1970) has been compiled by

J. Volf. But in the period of nearly ninety years which have passed since the discovery of the wild horse only two monographs aimed at a comprehensive discussion of the subject have appeared. One is W. W. Salensky's work *Equus Przewalskii Polj*, published in Saint Petersburg in 1902, which came out in English in 1907 with an introduction by J. C. Ewart, and the other, Erna Mohr's *Das Urwildpferd*, Booklet No 249 of the Neue Brahm-Bücherei; Wittenberg, 1959. A revised edition of this book was published in English in 1971, entitled *The Asiatic Wild Horse*.

Salensky's work is the best known among English readers, but unfortunately even at the time when it was written it was a rather poor work. The author was not a mammologist and was commissioned to write the book merely because he was a member of the Academy of Sciences. There are innumerable inaccuracies in the book and even errors of fact, all springing from the author's lack of expertise in a specialist field. E. A. Büchner, leading researcher of the Saint Petersburg Museum of Zoology, the zoologist of the first expeditions sent out to capture wild horses, and thus the scientist who might be expected to know more about the Mongolian wild horse than anyone else, sharply criticized Salensky's work in 1903. However, his forty-page-long paper was published only in Russian, so has hardly found its way into foreign readers' hands.

Erna Mohr's book, on the other hand, is a fine example of what a good monograph on a wild animal species should be. The author spent her whole life studying Przevalsky horses, and was personally acquainted with virtually every Mongolian wild horse in the zoos of Western and Central Europe. It was she too who set up the Stud Book of wild horses.

It was only after the publication of the German version of Mohr's books that the two symposia on Przevalsky horses took place. The papers presented there considerably advanced our knowledge, and opened up numerous new areas of study, for example into chromosome structures. Since then a thorough work summarizing the results of research on the Przevalsky horse in the Soviet Union, containing a lot of new data and corrections, has appeared. And the Hungarian entomologist Z. Kaszab has again encountered wild horses, believed to be extinct in their natural habitat, in South-West Mongolia.

For all these reasons, a new monograph on the Mongolian wild horse seems now to be timely. In my work I have relied in the first place on previous monographs, but I have brought them up to date with the results of the symposia, and the findings of the most recent research on the direct predecessors of the Mongolian wild horse. I have studied the Soviet material and made the necessary corrections to the accounts of the first Mongolian wild horses introduced to Europe. And finally I have included the results of my own research work in this field. The sections on the occurrence of the Mongolian wild horse in the folklore of Mongolia and of Central Asia in general; on the role it played in the emergence of the domestic horse and the part it has in the mythology of Central Asian peoples, are basically new. As the book is intended not as a text book but as information for the general public interested in zoology, I have not included technical detail except where this is indispensable.

For their kind permission to use data, photographs and line drawings in my work I should like to extend my thanks to Prof Dr C. G. Anghi, Budapest; Dr I. Erdélyi, Budapest; Dr M. Gábori, Budapest ; Dr I. M. Gromov, Leningrad; Dr

Z. Kaszab, Budapest; Dr G. Lükö, Kiskunfélegyháza; Dr M. Teichert, Halle and Dr J. Volf, Prague. I am particularly obliged to the Board of the Institute of Zoology of the Soviet Academy of Sciences for letting me have the photographs of the holotype of the Mongolian wild horse, and of the photograph taken of Colonel Przevalsky in 1876, before his second expedition to Central Asia. This latter photograph is published for the first time.

I am also grateful to Dr G. Nobis, Duisburg, for allowing me to peruse the relevant sections of his monograph entitled *Zur Stammesgeschichte der Wildpferde im Eiszeitalter und das Problem ihrer Domestikation in der Nacheiszeit* to be published shortly by Böhlau Verlag, Cologne. Finally my warmest thanks go to Dr Gy. Kara, Miss A. Sárközy and Miss K. Melles, associates of the Central Asia Institute of the Loránd Eötvös University, Budapest, for their helpfulness in selecting and translating Mongolian texts.

# INTRODUCTION

On June 30th 1966 a heavily loaded overland-car was climbing up the pass between the mountains Adj Bogd ul and Takhiyn Shaara nuru. Inside were Hungarian zoologist Z. Kaszab, his Mongol colleague Namkhaydorj Balgan, and a driver. Kaszab is an entomologist and he knows Mongolia very well, for he has travelled systematically all over the country in search of insect life. This was his fourth and final expedition.

He had set out from Ulan Bator, the capital of Mongolia, on June 17th and was on his way to West Mongolia. This territory is not unknown to European explorers. Since Colonel Przevalsky's first expeditions in the 'seventies and 'eighties of the last century, numerous explorers had visited the region, which was a veritable paradise for zoologists—and is one even today. Its fauna differs not only from that of Mongolia but also from that of the territories east of it, for it has several species not to be found anywhere else. For example, here live the Mongolian beaver (in the flood-area of the River Bulgan), and the wild camel, as well as the last species of wild horses, the Przevalsky horse. If we add to these the gazelle, the saiga-antelope and the kulan (the half-ass), we realise why a zoologist will undergo considerable hardship for the chance to study there.

17

Access to the area was relatively easy in the last century because it was quite near the boundaries of the then empire of the Tsar, and one of the two chief caravan routes leading from Siberia to China crossed the region. This was the route from Barnaul in Siberia to Peking, stretching eastward through West Mongolia via the city of Kobdo, then along the basin of the great lakes and the Lake Valley between the Hangai and the Altai, or across the Mongol Altai and the Gobi of Djungharia, finally to reach the Tien san.

Today—as evinced by Kaszab's experiences—it is much more complicated. It is true that the traveller need no longer rely on the slowly trudging camel, since he can use a car. On the other hand, to get to West Mongolia he must now start from Ulan Bator, which means that he has a journey of at least 1,000 km across country where there are no built roads at all. "Certain road-sections are impassable in rainy weather or when the snow has melted. After a shower or several days of rain the rivers flood to such an extent that one cannot cross them by car. In other places sand hampers movement. In many places, particularly in the south-western, uninhabited region, there are no roads of any kind. The petrol and water supply also causes great difficulties, nor is there any possibility to buy provisions while travelling," wrote Kaszab, who—with his escorts— could reach the goal he had set himself only by straining himself to the utmost.

In the evening of June 29th Kaszab reached the boundary of the Djungharian Gobi, the goal, so much longed for, of his expedition. Spurred on by the researcher's impatient excitement he struck tents early in the morning, and set out to climb the pass across the mountains, aiming to reach the valley of the rivulet Bidj gol, the planned site of his next camp, the same day. This, however, was by no means an easy job, for there was no trace of any road. Luckily he had a contour map of the area, by the help of which he was able to find among the dry river beds the road leading to the pass. The overland-car had to struggle hard to climb the pass, but the panorama spreading before the travellers' eyes compensated them for their trouble. Virtually the whole mountain range unrolled before them. From there their course went steep upwards to the plateau, almost completely flat, of a place called Takhiyn Shaara nuru, at an altitude of about 2,000 metres. Then it led to the dry bed of the river Tukhumin khundi, at some places one kilometre wide, flanked by precipitous mountains. On the bottom of the river bed were scattered here and there small hillocks of sand and heaps of stones with tamarisk shrubs or saxaul bushes, sometimes even reeds on their tops, indicating the presence of subsoil water.

The weather was rather cool with a strong north-westerly headwind. Quite suddenly a group of galloping animals appeared a few kilometres before the car. At once Kaszab's Mongolian colleague exclaimed: "Wild horses!" He had several times seen Przevalsky horses in their natural habitat, and he recognized them at once. To be certain, Kaszab needed binoculars. But a thorough examination through them assured him that they were wild horses and not kulans (half-asses). These were an exciting few seconds, for they had indeed discovered Przevalsky horses, not seen in free nature by human eyes for several years and thus assumed, in their natural habitat, to be already extinct.

Kaszab and his companions tried to approach the group of horses. As far as the conditions of the soil allowed them to, they tried to follow them, chasing them at a speed of approximately forty kilometres per hour for about twenty minutes, but they were unable to diminish the distance separating them from the animals.

In the beginning the wild horses—with the exception of one individual—were galloping in one mass, and thus could not be counted. But later they scattered and could be counted. The group contained eight horses. The animal galloping at the end, as if it were a rear-guard, was a stallion, the other seven were mares. There was no young animal, or foal, in the group.

The chase went on for ten–twelve kilometres, but finally the animals vanished at a bend. Kaszab tried to take photographs. Unfortunately, in one of his cameras all frames of the film had been exposed and in the other only two frames remained. In the excitement of the chase and in the hope of getting nearer to the animals he did not stop the car to put in a new film, so he could take only two colour transparencies of the galloping herd, one with his normal lens and the other with a 100mm tele-objective. In the latter shot the animals are fairly well discernible, though they cannot be identified with full certainty. However, the size of the hoof-prints shows clearly that the animals were really horses and not half-asses. Thus it has been ascertained that the last species of wild horse has not become extinct in free nature, nor has it disappeared from the territory of Mongolia. Though very rare, it survives in areas uninhabited and undisturbed by man, by grazing in territories where it can find at least the minimum quantity of water.

## THE EVOLUTION OF HORSES

The equids living today represent the summit of a very long evolutionary process. This process started at least sixty million years ago, and although it took place in two continents—Eurasia and America—at times parallel and at other times at different stages in different localities, it has been clarified very well in practically all its details. There is hardly any other group of mammals whose evolution is as clear to us as is that of horses.

The first ancestor of equids, the *Hyracotherium*, found as early as 1839 at a site in Kent, differed to such an extent, both in the form of its skull and in its dentition, from present-day horses that nobody thought of establishing any link between the two. Richard Owen, who described it, considered it a hyrax-like animal; that is where its name was derived from. Darwin's evolution theory had to spread among paleontologists before one could even think of setting up evolution lines. Meanwhile the number of finds also increased, but each was a solitary datum, and to order them into a connected series of evolution was, we may well say, the first touchstone of Darwin's theory. Thomas Henry Huxley, a close friend of Darwin's, was the first to succeed in this in 1872, and he was followed by the Russian paleontologist Vladimir Kovalevsky in 1873.

The two eminent paleontologists admitted themselves that the evolutionary series they had set up was incomplete. The gaps were filled later, first of all by American paleontologists. Even then however the evolutionary series *Palaeotherium—Anchitherium—Hipparion—Equus* had a grave defect: its starting point was missing. The *Hyracotherium* was not recognized as the earliest form of equids until it was finally put in its right place by the American Cope some years later.

The group of mammals from which the equids emerged was the order of the *Condylarthra*. It appeared in the Paleocene and became extinct before the end of the Eocene Age. The genus from which the equids originated was the *Phenacodus*, which came into being in the early Eocene, that is about fifty-five million years ago. The *Phenacodus* was a mammal, much undifferentiated, possessing the qualities both of carnivorous and herbivorous mammals, though it was rather like the latter. It was by and large the shape of a fox, and in size somewhere between the dog and the horse. It was a five-toed animal, walking almost on its sole; and it had a small head and a long, bulky tail. Its five toes were characteristic of primitive mammals. But it had a hoof at the end of each toe, and this was a feature pointing to the future. Only the three middle toes of the five touched the ground, the two flanking them—the thumb and the little toe—remaining only rudimentary. The proportions of the limbs indicate that the *Phenacodus* could not have been a very swift runner.

The skull of the *Phenacodus* was also rather undifferentiated and represented the type of primitive mammals. Its brain was far less developed than that of today's horse. The dentition, too, showed numbers characteristic of primitive mammals: both in the lower and upper row of teeth there were three incisors, one canine, four premolars and three molars; thus it had altogether forty-four teeth. In comparison the dentition of most present mammals comprises fewer: a stallion has, in general, forty teeth and a mare thirty-six, although exceptionally, by way of atavism, the original first premolars will appear in a rudimentary form, the so-called wolf teeth. Moreover, the *Phenacodus* had no diastema between the incisors and premolars, which even the most primitive equids have; and its canines were like those of predatory animals. Though the anterior premolars were simple, the next ones and the molars got progressively larger, and consisted of several cusps.

In size the *Hyracotherium** (or its relative on the American continent, the *Eohippus*) was very close to the *Phenacodus*. The smallest species of this extraordinarily variable ancestor of the horse could have had a withersheight of 25 cm, and the biggest was no taller than 50 cm.

The *Hyracotherium* represented a significant evolutionary step. As far as its characteristics were concerned, it was, no doubt, quite close to the primitive condylarth mammals and must therefore have somewhat resembled a rabbit. However, the soles had already risen considerably from the ground, and instead of the *Phenacodus'* five toes it had only four on the fore-feet and three on the hind-feet, with tiny hooves on each of the toes. On the fore-feet only the first toe became rudimentary, on the hind ones both the first and the fifth, with only a small bone remaining in the place of each under the skin. The middle toe bore the chief part

*(The name *Eohippus* would at the same time be much easier to remember and more logical, since its first part indicates that the animal came into being during the Eocene, and the second that it is an equid, since hippos means horse in Greek. However, observing the strict rules of the nomenclature of zoology, we must adhere to the older name *Hyracotherium*).

of the body's weight, but the second and fourth toes, though somewhat less developed, also helped in carrying it. The skull closely resembled that of the *Phenacodus*, and the number of teeth was also forty-four. However, the diastema had appeared, the canines were small, and although the premolars were still definitely cusped, on the molars the cusps were beginning to be reduced to crests. This was definitely a herbivorous animal's dentition.

The next link in the chain of evolution was the *Mesohippus* of the Oligocene (about thirty-five million years ago). It was an equid of about 60 cm average withers-height, and had three toes on its fore-feet as well as its hind-feet. In its looks, in the proportions of its body and its limbs it was much nearer to present-day horses than the *Hyracotherium*. Its dentition, too, showed a strong development: the premolars—with the exception of the first—had become similar to the molars, as in present-day horses. Then the late-Oligocene *Miohippus* strongly resembled the *Mesohippus*—it was only larger.

From this point onwards the evolution of the horse became more intricate. The *Anchitherium*, emerging from the *Miohippus* and surviving up to the Miocene (about twenty-five million years ago), proved to be a collateral, as did the *Hypohippus*. The chief evolution line continued in the *Parahippus* and the *Merychippus*, which had emerged about the middle of the Pliocene.

A complete change from browsing to grazing took place in the *Merychippus*. This was concomitant on the one hand with the growing height of the crown of the teeth; and on the other with the evolution of enamel ridges from the condylarth cusps and the appearance of a cement substance to support the enamel ridges. Thus the characteristic dentition of equids had emerged, and changed only insignificantly later on. Although the *Merychippus* species showed great variability, a general increase of size can be observed and certain species reached a withers-height of one metre. In its skull and body form, too, the *Merychippus* was nearer to our modern horse. Although it still had three toes, the middle toe got markedly developed, whereas the two flanking it atrophied. In a state of rest the middle toe alone bore the weight of the body, the other two working like springs to quicken movement. The *Merychippus* thus represented the most profound qualitative transformation in the evolution of equids, and Zittel, the eminent German paleontologist, accordingly considered this genus the first member of the equids in the strict meaning of the term.

Evolving from the *Merychippus* and different from it chiefly in features of dentition, the *Hipparion* and *Neohipparion* again proved to be dead-ends and became extinct by the end of the Pliocene (which began about ten million and ended about one million years ago) and the beginning of the Pleistocene. The other branch originating from the *Merychippus*, the *Pliohippus*, represented the continued line of evolution. It was with this change that one-toed horses appeared on our Earth, although in early species of this genus rudimentary side-toes still occurred. In developed *Pliohippus* species, the memory of the side-toes is indicated only by pointed, fish-bone-like bones on the two sides of the metapodials. This is the case with recent horses too, although sometimes individuals occur with a rudimentary toe on both sides of the end of their feet by way of atavism: this was the case, for instance, with Alexander the Great's saddle horse, Bucephalus ("the ox-headed"), which, after long and faithful service, finally perished in distant India; or with Julius Caesar's favourite saddle horse.

The skull of the *Pliohippus* is also much like that of the *Equus,* which name represents the highest grade in the evolution of equids, and differs from the latter first of all by its marked facial hollows. The only essential difference in its dentition is that the upper molars, on account of their uneven lengthwise growth, are strongly bent.

Out of the *Pliohippus* the genus *Equus* evolved some time about the upper end of the Pliocene and spread over the Earth very quickly. It differed from its predecessor first and foremost in the size of its body and by its skull form and dentition. It is interesting to note that although the *Equus* genus in the broader meaning of the term (that is to say, the equids) came into being on the continent of America and spread from there to all other continents with the exception of Australia, it soon became extinct in its place of origin and did not continue to evolve there.

At the beginning of the Pleistocene the *Equus* genus got divided into four subgenera. The zebras (*Hippotigris* = tiger-horse) spread over the southern and south-eastern part of Africa; and the asses (*Asinus*) occupied the eastern and northern edges of the same continent. Half-asses (*Hemionus*) reached the broad strip of Asia stretching from Arabia to Mongolia, while the genuine horses (*Equus*) are to be found in territories lying to the north and west of the regions mentioned above. There was possibly another, a fifth subgenus too, the *Hydruntinus,* occupying a place somewhere between asses and half-asses (some authors count them as asses), resembling the former in its dentition and the latter in its limbs. This animal, which used to live in the southern part of Europe, in south-west Asia and in Africa, became extinct in the first half of the Neolithic period.

These distribution areas of the subgenera of present

equids more or less represent the circumstances of the early Holocene. Earlier, in the Pleistocene, there had been remarkable changes in distribution, depending mostly on the fluctuations of the climate. Thus in the course of a westward movement of Asian steppe fauna, the half-asses reached the territory of today's Germany; and at another time, when the climate became warmer, the *Hydruntinus* found its way far north. Large territories are still completely unexplored from this point of view and may have quite a number of surprises in store for us.

The distribution areas of the subgenera of equids often met, and there were overlaps. Thus for example the distribution area of asses partly overlapped in the south with that of the zebras, as did the distribution area of half-asses with that of horses in the north. However in spite of the fact that among artificial conditions individuals of different subgenera can be crossed, in nature cross-breeding never occurs.

We can now summarize the purposes of the changes taking place in the course of the evolution of equids. The changes in the skull were necessary to accommodate an increasingly developed—and therefore larger—brain, in relation to other organs. As G. G. Simpson, the excellent American paleontologist, put it, although the *Eohippus,* the miniature horse, may have been a charming little animal, it could not have become a real pet, because compared with today's horses it was extraordinarily stupid. The changes in the teeth ensured the animals' shifts from omnivorous eating to browsing, then to eating soft-stemmed plants, and finally to grazing. The changes in stature, and in the structure and proportion of the limbs (among which we have dealt here only with those affecting the ends of the feet) were destined to ensure greater speed. On the other

hand, horses had to pay for their quicker movements by
losing the ability to move their limbs sideways; however
they did not need this ability as their evolution further
advanced.

The following table shows the phylogenic tree of equids
and its formation in the Old World and in the New:

| Period | Eurasia | America |
|---|---|---|
| Eocene | Hyracotherium | Hyracotherium (Eohippus) |
| Oligocene | | Mesohippus <br> Miohippus |
| Miocene | Anchitherium ← <br> Hypohippus ← | Parahippus |
| Pliocene | Hipparion ← <br> Stylohipparion | Hipparion ← Merychippus <br> Neohipparion  Pliohippus |
| Pleistocene | Stylohipparion  Equus ← <br> Equus | Equus |

——————→ *Chief line of evolution*
------------→ *collateral lines*

# HORSES OF THE ICE AGE

From now on we will be dealing only with true horses (*Equus* subgenus). About the earliest part of their history, which took place in the Pleistocene, there reigned up to quite recent times enormous confusion. This was largely because the horse being the domestic animal perhaps nearest to man's heart, many people cherished the idea of studying its evolution and history; yet each worked separately, in a limited local context. Each had access to relatively few bones—few in comparison with the total discovered—found at a few sites. And no researcher had access to another's results. Thus theories about the evolution of the horse sprang up like mushrooms. Their authors could easily conceive hypotheses, for they had no opportunity to test and reject them against *all* the evidence. Consequently horse species of the Pleistocene, or at least their denominations, also sprang up like mushrooms. In recent years their number had risen to over a hundred.

The eminent German zoologist G. Nobis attempted to create order out of this chaos. Since he himself had been engaged in the attempts described above, he realized in the 'sixties that there was only one way out of the confusion: to have one author study all the Pleistocene and early Holocene horses of Eurasia, the scene of the final phase of

29

the evolution of horses. What was needed was a single homogeneous study, from a single point of view. And this is what he proceeded to undertake. As a result of his research he was able to conclude that side by side with the zebra-like horses of the early Pleistocene (which, however, were not zebras but the common ancestors of horses, zebras, asses and half-asses), large horses had also evolved. These latter survived into the middle-Pleistocene, although by then medium-sized or small horses played the leading role. By the end of the Pleistocene large horses had completely disappeared and only a single medium-sized species was to be found in the whole of Eurasia. Nobis called this—using the oldest name of such wild horses, first used in 1785—*Equus ferus*. Thus it is that *Equus* is the common name not only of the Holocene species but also of the present Eurasian wild horse.

In European and Asian cave paintings, reliefs and other works of art of the Pleistocene period wild horses very often appear. They were represented not for joy in their appearance, but as a magic to influence the hunt. In prehistoric man's belief the picture of an animal meant the living, actual animal, and possessing the picture was tantamount to possessing the animal itself. In Paleolithic conditions the capture or domestication of animals was still out of the question, so possession could only mean killing the animal. Thus to represent it by painting it on the wall would contribute to its killing and to the success of the hunt.

Such representations in caves are known, first of all, in the Mediterranean region, in the famous caves of Southern France and Spain, though in addition to these there are others in other regions of Eurasia. It is a common feature of all representations of animals of the Paleolithic and

Mesolithic periods that they are extraordinarily realistic, so much so that numerous paleontologists have attempted to identify species of horses and even subspecies from these pictures. There is however hardly any point in trying to do this. As Ucko and Rosenfeld have clearly shown in their book on the art of Paleolithic rock paintings, there was even at that time a certain "artistic licence" which permitted significant variations in the representation of animals externally similar. Besides, the Paleolithic artist, though viewing the animal he represented with a hunter's eye, could hardly be expected to take the point of view of the zoologist engaged with systematics, and he did not always emphasize the features the zoologist would have considered important. In any case paleontology, since it deals with animals of times long past, is a branch of the science of biology, so the material of its investigations must be primarily biological; that is, the teeth, bones and other animal remains. To answer questions that cannot be answered by the examination of biological material only, the paleontologist may use other sources, but only in order to support and complete conclusions established on biological grounds.

Among Central and West European representations of Pleistocene horses, particularly those originating from the end of the period, we can often find pictures reminiscent of the Przevalsky horse. This is by no means surprising; on the other hand, no sweeping inferences can be drawn from the fact. Too many people have asserted that these representations are splendid proof that the Mongolian wild horse found its way to Europe in the Pleistocene. As Nobis points out, this indicates only that among the uniform Eurasian wild horses of the late Pleistocene—one of whose extremely diminished edge-forms the Przevalsky horse was—there were a great many whose skull form resembled that of today's Mongolian wild horses.

We know some representations of horses from the Paleolithic period of Central and Northern Asia too. Such for example are the upper Paleolithic rock drawings of Shishkino, the region whence the river Lena springs. Hancar definitely thought he could recognize in them the Przevalsky horse.

## THE ORIGIN AND EVOLUTION OF THE
## MONGOLIAN WILD HORSE

In 1878 Colonel N. M. Przevalsky presented the fell and
skull of a wild horse to the Saint Petersburg Zoological
Museum of the Russian Academy of Sciences. The eminent
explorer, who had returned in that year from his second
expedition to Central Asia, had received the fell and the
skull from A. K. Tikhanov, stationmaster of Saisansk on the
Russian border. The general opinion used to prevail that
the Colonel was given the present at the end of his second
expedition; but in their extraordinarily thorough monograph on the investigation and breeding of Przevalsky
horses in the Soviet Union, Garrutt, Sokolov and Salesskaya
declared that it was not impossible that the skull and fell
had been obtained during the first expedition. The animal
had been killed by Kirghisian hunters in the desert of South
Djungharia.

No doubt the Colonel was fully aware of the value of
the gift. During his travels he had seen wild horses himself, and several times tried to kill one of them, but he had
always failed. In his book on his third expedition he wrote
the following: "During my whole stay there I met only
two herds of horses. My escort and I shot at the herds, but
in vain. With its tail raised high and its neck arched, the
stallion whizzed away, the whole herd following it. We

could not follow them because we lost trace immediately. On another occasion we succeeded in stalking them from the side, but suddenly one of the animals noticed me. At once they galloped away at the top of their speed and vanished from my sight."

The fell and skull were transferred to I.S. Poliakov, conservator of the Museum of Zoology, who—on the basis of the remains—declared a new species of wild horse discovered. In the Colonel's honour he called the species Przevalsky horse (its scientific name *Equus przewalskii*). The mounted fell and skull—as type-specimen of the new species—are to be seen even today in the Institute of Zoology of the Soviet Academy of Sciences in Leningrad.

There is a small but interesting point in Poliakov's description of the type. At that time (1881) he estimated the age of the animal to have been three years. In 1891 I. D. Tcherskij did not accept this determination of age and now Garrutt and his two co-authors, having thoroughly examined the teeth, ascertained that the age indicated by Poliakov was indeed wrong, for the animal may have been only fifteen months old.

The scientific description of the Przevalsky horse created a sensation among zoologists. At the time when the news was published there were still wild horses on the steppes of South Russia, and the discovery of a Mongolian wild horse stirred up a great controversy among the experts. There were zoologists who simply did not believe that the Przevalsky horse was really a horse and not a half-ass, a kulan, an animal which at that time was to be found in huge masses in Djungharia and in other regions of Central Asia. However, the majority of specialists accepted Poliakov's contention and the years to come confirmed them in their judgement.

The greatest problem was to decide whether the Mongolian wild horse was really an independent species, what its origin had been and what its relationship with the early wild horses of Eurasia. In this respect there existed innumerable views up to quite recent times. It would not be worth while to enumerate them all, for only a few were based on scientific examination, the rest on mere guesswork.

To answer the three questions—they are closely connected with one another—we have to go back to the horses that could surely have been the starting points of the Przevalsky horse, namely, the wild horses of the end of the Ice Age, and the beginning of the Holocene respectively.

We have to recall that the Eurasian group of horses at the end of the Ice Age, animals considered by Nobis to belong to one species, comprised wild horses variable in size from small to medium. Nobis thought that the medium-sized ones were in the majority, while the small ones lived at the two ends of the distribution area, namely in Western Europe and in Central Asia. What was the cause of this diminution? According to Nobis, nothing but the unfavourable environment. In the case of Mongolian wild horses we may rightly speak of an unfavourable environment: horses are not animals of the steppe-desert; they have been pushed back there only by the advance of man. That the Mongolian wild horse is indeed a small-size descendant of larger wild horses is shown by the size of its teeth, which are strikingly large in proportion to its skull; for it is a well-known fact in paleontology that in the case of such transformations teeth do not behave as plastically as the skull, and the bones of the trunk in particular, do. Teeth respond to changes of environment more slowly.

Thus, in Nobis' opinion the Mongolian wild horse is not

an independent species but a subspecies of the uniform Eurasian wild horse (*Equus ferus*), a subspecies he called by the scientific name *Equus ferus przewalskii*. He considers the wild horse of South Russia, the tarpan, also to be a subspecies and denominates it *Equus ferus gmelini*.

The Przevalsky horse may have had very close connexions with the rest of the wild horse population of Central Asia. In addition to bones, a most interesting complete carcass of a horse was found recently, which provides positive evidence of this.

In the autumn of 1969 Soviet newspapers reported that workers digging a shaft for gold-washing at the River Indigirka in Yakutia had made a remarkable find. From a depth of eight—nine metres, the zone of permanent frost, they brought to light the complete and well-conserved carcass of a horse. O. V. Yegorov, a senior researcher of the Yakutian Academy of Sciences, who had taken part in the excavation, considered the find to be 15,000–20,000 years old.

"The find is unique of its kind in the whole world," the short item of news declared, "and may be interesting not only for Soviet scientists but for foreign researchers as well. This find may give information about what the ancestors of today's horses were like, a question strongly debated. In the frozen soil the animal was preserved very well and it is reminiscent of the wild Przevalsky horse, extant even today. On the other hand, it also shows features characteristic of horses that lived some hundred years ago on the northern shore of the Black Sea and on the steppes of the Transcaspian region. When the cold weather sets in the find can be transported to the Zoological Institute in Leningrad."

It is to be hoped that the horse's carcass has indeed got to
Leningrad and that the results of a full scientific investigation will soon be published. It will almost certainly provide
us with information about the earlier Asian distribution of
the Przevalsky horse.*

It is already evident that the Przevalsky horse used to
be distributed in areas inhabited by the Kirghiz and the
Kazakh. As a matter of fact, the former have a separate
word for the wild horse. In a letter M. S. Yurin, who was
born in Bashkiria and lived there up to 1930, informed the
Soviet zoologist V. G. Heptner that in 1903-4 he had seen
a wild horse captured in the Kirghizian Mountains. It was
a powerful animal, with long, wavy hair, a short, erect
mane and a sparsely haired, short tail. This description fits
the Mongolian wild horse very well, and suggests that the
animal occurred there too.

The situation in Tibet is not so unequivocal. It is possible
that there used to live—at least in the northern part of
Tibet—Przevalsky horses, although so far we have not had
any concrete data on this. Given the situation there, it is
by no means surprising that no remains have been discovered to date.

According to Heptner the distribution area of Asian
wild horses was fantastically vast even in historical eras.
Northwards it stretched to the 55th degree of latitude, and

*It is of course by no means rare for animals' carcasses frozen in the
ice to be discovered in the tundras of Siberia. The famous carcass of
the Berezovka mammoth in the Zoological Institute in Leningrad was
washed out by the water from the frozen layers of a river wall. In
Tsarist times many carcasses did not find their way to research
institutes because dogs and foxes ate them up on the spot. It was also
from such frozen layers that the horse mummies of the famous kurgans
of the fifth century B.C. of Pazyryk were brought to light. Some of
them, too, are to be found at the Zoological Institute in Leningrad.

eastwards to the 85th degree of longitude. Southwards the Caucasus and the Caspian Sea were its boundaries, which run from the latter's north-eastern shores through Lake Aral and Lake Balkhas to the northern foot-hills of the Altai. It seems to be probable too that westwards Przevalsky horses were distributed as far as the Ural, and made contact with the South Russian tarpans in the regions between the Ural and the Volga.

By now their distribution area has been narrowed down very considerably, restricted as it is to the Takhiyn Shaara nuru Mountains, and certain areas of Takhiyn-nus and Djungharia adjacent to them, on both sides of the Mongolian-Chinese frontier. That they have been pushed back is not simply the consequence of increase in human population. The fact that nomadic peoples and their constantly increasing herds had occupied all the watering places, also played a part. Although the wild horse can survive without water for two days or three, it soon perishes from thirst. In recent years the number of Przevalsky horses has decreased so much that the expeditions launched by Peking zoo in 1955–7 were unable to capture a single animal. When in 1966 Kaszab encountered his group of eight wild horses, not one wild horse had been seen in Mongolia for several years. Since then their number seems to have grown, for recently several reports mention sightings of wild horses in the south-western part of the country.

How many Przevalsky horses live in the wild today? This is a question very hard to answer. According to the Soviet zoologist Bannikov there were in 1958 not more than forty, although he pointed out that on account of the extraordinarily difficult terrain all attempts at counting them, or even estimating their number, might only result in quite inaccurate figures. According to the Mongolian D. E. Dagwa there might have been in 1954 as many as between fifty and a hundred, but their number has markedly decreased. It is highly probable that nobody would dare even to guess at their present number.

# DOMESTIC HORSES' BLOOD IN
## PRZEVALSKY HORSES?

No sooner had the type specimen acquired by Colonel
Przevalsky been published, than the Mongolian wild horse
became very popular among mammologists. Soon a number of institutions wanted to obtain Przevalsky horses, dead
or alive, and several expeditions set out for Central Asia.
For geographical reasons the Russians were first to launch
such expeditions, but soon C. Hagenbeck, the hunter and
dealer in animals, perhaps the greatest of all times, too
appeared on the scene, for he had a flair for the business
side of the matter.

The first Europeans not only to see the Przevalsky horse
but successfully to hunt it were the Russian Grum-
Grshmailo brothers, who travelled in the western part of
the Chinese Empire in 1889-90. During their expedition
they killed four wild horses—three stallions and a mare—
and sent the four fells and the skulls of the three stallions
(one together with the incomplete skeleton) to the Saint
Petersburg Academy of Sciences. These have been preserved
to this day at the Zoological Institute in Leningrad.

One fell and skull acquired by V. I. Roborovski's and
P. K. Koslov's expedition also found its way to the same
place. Another one was presented to the University of
Moscow and the third to the zoological gallery of the

Jardin des Plantes in Paris. They are to be found in the three institutions today.

At a later date the Russian Consul of Urga, J. P. Shishmarev, presented a fell with the skull belonging to it to the Zoological Institute in Saint Petersburg.

Having examined all these finds together, I. D. Tcherskij (1891) confirmed Poliakov's opinion, that the Przevalsky horse was a real horse and not a half-ass, or a cross-breed of half-ass and domestic horse. Tcherskij did not however investigate the question of whether the Przevalsky horse was a genuine wild horse or a feral domestic horse. Only later investigations gave an answer to this question—first those of A. A. Tikhomirov (1898–1902)—at a time when zoologists had not only come to know the Mongolian wild horse better through the wild horses imported to European and American zoos, but had also, thanks to lucky finds, learned more about the wild horses of the Ice Age and thus found a reliable ground for comparisons. The answer was that the Przevalsky horse was indeed an original wild horse and not a feral domestic horse.

It is another question whether the blood of domestic horses could have found its way into that of Mongolian wild horses, and whether it actually did so. No doubt, it could have done. There are examples in the case not only of horses but of every other domestic animal, of individuals from a domestic species cross-breeding with individuals from the wild. With respect to cattle we have very good osteological proofs of such cross-breeding from the Neolithic age. Bastards coming into being in this way can be very well distinguished from wild cattle, for the former lose the strictly determined proportions characteristic of the latter. Prophesies in the Old Testament about animals also mention the occurrence of such cross-breeding. In the

41

case of pigs in countries of the Balkans, where herds of domestic swine are driven into the mountains in spring and taken back along with their progeny to the villages only in autumn, such cross-breeds are frequent even today. The question poses problems to the breeders of reindeer too, because the products of cross-breeding will often inherit a great deal of the wild father's vehemence; they are often vicious and are difficult to handle. As late as the beginning of our century South American horse-breeders were in a quandary, because feral stallions would carry away mares. The situation was similar in nineteenth-century Southern Russia, where lonely tarpan stallions carried away mares from domestic herds to form a harem for themselves. Horse-breeders, of course, looked askance at such occurrences and this was one of the causes of the excessive hunting of the tarpan, which finally led to the complete extinction of wild horses in Southern Russia.

When the first Mongolian wild horses captured alive reached Europe it soon turned out that some of them were not full-blooded wild horses but products of cross-breeding between the wild horse and the domestic one. It is highly probable that the Mongolian agents of European animal traders, and the Mongolian hunters themselves, were businessmen clever enough to capture the bastards and sell them to the merchants instead of the wild horses, which would be more difficult to catch. Nor is it impossible that now and then they sold bastards from herds of domestic horses, pretending they were wild horses. Since, at the end of the last century and the beginning of this one, we knew very little about the Przevalsky horse, the traders easily accepted these animals as wild horses. It was only later that specialist zoologists ascertained whether they were pure-blooded wild horses or not.

There were for instance two bastards among the first consignment of Mongolian mares to reach Europe. They arrived in 1899 or 1900 at the estate of the horse-breeder F. E. Falz-Fein at Askania Nova in South Russia. Antonius, the eminent Austrian horse specialist, found at least one in the second group imported by Hagenbeck, which reached Europe in 1902.

Truth to tell, all the conditions were present in Mongolia for the bastardization of domestic horses with wild ones. In the wake of wars, of greater and lesser marauding expeditions, there were always disrupted herds of domestic horses, which ran away and became feral. In his book about his third expedition to Central Asia Przevalsky wrote the following in 1883:

> "The Mongols have told me that there are still feral horses on the Tüngheri. These horses escaped when the Dunghans devastated Ala-Shan in 1869. Since then these horses have been wandering about, living at their will. They are most cautious, and go to drink only at night or to watering places not visited by people. But the Mongols killed many of them by ambush, or captured them with lassos. Now there are only some dozen of them alive; most of them have their haunt in the Gankhay-tzi Mountains some 40 kilometres from the Bayan-bulük well. In that place there is a small salt-water pond and there are two wells, at which the feral horses drink. In all probability they too will be killed or captured by the Mongols after a time. In 1873 we also saw five such horses at the Bayan-bulük well."

Indeed, under the conditions of extensive animal breeding in Mongolia, it often happens today that domestic horses go feral. It is enough if one of the nomads, due to

43

illness or some other reason, relaxes his supervision of a part of his herd. On such occasions smaller or bigger groups of horses get easily separated from the herd and roam about the steppe. If they encounter a wild stallion it will challenge the domestic ones and—by his greater strength, hardness and cleverness—destroy even the strongest. D. E. Dagwa, himself a native of South-West Mongolia, a region to which wild horses have recently withdrawn, knows of several similar cases and, as far as he knows, it was always the Przevalsky stallions that were the victors in such combats. He described one occurrence as follows (1954):

"An Arate neglected a part of his herd and these horses soon became feral. After a few months the animals did not allow anyone to approach them and after a short time they disappeared in the Takhiyn Shaara-nuru Mountains. This happened between 1949 and 1952. In 1952 a lonely Przevalsky stallion met the group of horses. The stallion of the feral herd, an animal the Arates knew to be very strong, started a fight with the stranger. Later the feral stallion's carcass was found on the spot where the combat had taken place. Its legs were broken, its ears torn off, and large parts of the skin together with the flesh were torn off the body. Evidently, his internal injuries were similarly grave. The wild stallion became the head of the group, with which it remained up to the end of 1952."

It is not only under such tragic circumstances that hybrids between wild horses and domestic ones come into being. It has also happened more than once that lonely domestic mares have gone astray and been covered by Przevalsky stallions. The mares later returned to the herd and gave birth to their foals there.

44

Such cases do not seem to be everyday occurrences, for livestock is the foundation of the nomads' wealth and they try to protect it by any means. But it also appears to be doubtless that domestic horses' blood may occur in Przevalsky horses too. This, however, does not at all reduce their quality as genuine wild horses. It is hardly believable that any wild ancestor of domestic animals could be found today, without some of the domestic form's blood.

# PRZEWALSKII HORSES TODAY

## THE NAME OF THE MONGOLIAN WILD HORSE

As we know, Poliakov entered the Mongolian wild horse into the literature of zoology under the name of *Equus przewalskii*, in 1881. Later Noack wanted to separate a branch of Przevalsky horses by the name of *Equus hagenbecki*, as an independent species; whereas Hilzheimer on the other hand tried to identify the wild horses Pallas had described under the name of *Equus equiferus* with the Przevalsky horse. Heptner considered them a species identical with the tarpan and denominated them as a subspecies, *Equus przewalskii przewalskii*. In Nobis's opinion too the Mongolian wild horse is a subspecies, of the Late-Pleistocene–Early-Holocene Eurasian wild horse, and since the latter's oldest name is *Equus ferus*, he called the Przevalsky horse *Equus ferus przewalskii*.

In the international literature of zoology—unless the official Latin denomination is applied—the expression Przevalsky horse, Mongolian wild horse or *Urwildpferd* (original wild horse) are the names used. The last name is mostly used in German literature, to distinguish between original wild horses and those that have been "rebred" in experiments to "rebreed" ("reconstitute") wild horses from domestic ones that have been carried out in some German and Polish zoological gardens since the 1930s. Recently the name *Takhi*, derived from the Mongolian name of the Przevalsky horse, has also been gaining ground.

Occasionally the name *Tarpan* will also be used for the Mongolian wild horse, transferred from the name of the wild horse of Southern Russia, which still lived in the wild when the Mongolian horse was first discovered in the 1870s. Although Przevalsky was aware of the fact that the skull and fell he had received at Saisansk belonged to a new species of wild horse, he handed them over to the Russian Academy of Sciences as the remains of a tarpan.

According to Przevalsky the Kirghiz called the wild horse *Kirtag* (and not *Körtag* as Grevé mentioned in 1901), while the Mongolians called it *Take*. He also declared that the name of the kulan was *Surtag*. Brehm stated that the Kirghiz name for the wild horse was *Surtake*, and according to Poliakov it was *Surtaken*. Langkavel quoted *Kertag* as the Kirghiz and Tartar name of the wild horse, the Mongolian denomination being *Take* and *Statur*.

According to Falz-Fein (1930), in Mongolian, bay-coloured wild horses were called *Syrtach* and dark ones *Kurtach*, and in these names "Syr" means desert, "Kur" mountain and "tach" horse. Thus the two names mean both the habitat and the colour variant.

Many other authors indicate *Takhi* as the Mongolian name of the Przevalsky horse—and they seem to be nearest to truth, since in Mongolian folk-tales and folk-poetry—that is to say in their modern transcription in Roman letters—the wild horse always appears as *Takh*, whereas in ancient Mongolian it is called *Takhi*.

For the eye used to our present, contemporary domestic horse, the Przevalsky horse is a small animal, roughly the size of the Fjord horse, the Polish konik or the Russian panye horse. Its withers-height varies between 124 and 145 cm, and is 135 cm on the average. Its weight is between 250 and 300 kg.

The build on the other hand is powerful and massive. In proportion to the trunk the head is large, though rather short, and in comparison with the brain position of the skull the nasal part is long, usually straight in profile, though sometimes ram-nosed individuals occur. The forehead is broad and gently bulging, the jaw powerful and the masticatory muscles are particularly strongly developed on stallions—they lend strength to the formidable bites the fighting stallions inflict upon one another. The upper lip is somewhat longer than the lower and it sometimes overlaps it. The ears are small and pointed and the teeth are big, with a simple pattern of enamel.

The neck is short and broad, and is very muscular. So is the powerful, deep chest, whose length was set about 124 cm by Mohr (1959). The back is short, generally straight, the withers are flat, hardly protruding at all. The rump is flat and not furrowy, and compared with that of today's ideal domestic horse it is rather poor in muscular development.

On account of the deep trunk the legs are rather short and strong, though they are not thick-set. The hooves are round (thus they are not reminiscent of asses' as are the kulan's hooves) and they are relatively broad. Their horn substance is very good, for it should be borne in mind that the wild horse has to use its hooves on a dry, hard and sometimes stony terrain. On the inner side of each of the four legs there is a chestnut; on the forelegs this is above the carpal joint and on the hindlegs below the tarsal joints—unlike the chestnuts of asses and half-asses, which are to be found only on the forelegs.

The different segments of the spine of the Przevalsky horse show a very interesting formation. R. M. Stecher examined (1967) the skeletons of sixty-one Mongolian wild horses, and found that all of them had seven cervical vertebrae (the number of seven cervical vertebrae is the most common spinal feature among all species of mammals), thirty-three had eighteen dorsal vertebrae and twenty-eight had nineteen. Among the sixty-one skeletons eleven had five lumbar vertebrae, one had five-and-a-half and twenty-nine had six. In forty cases the sacrum consisted of five vertebrae, in ten cases of four, in three cases of four plus one, in one case of four-and-a-half, in four cases of five plus one, in one case of five-and-a-half and in one case of six sacral vertebrae. (In one case the sacrum was not complete.) Horses usually have six lumbar vertebrae; so the lumbar section of the Przevalsky horse seems to indicate a tendency towards shortening. The same tendency is shown on the sacrum. On the other hand the nineteen dorsal vertebrae to be found on each of twenty-eight animals appear to compensate for this shortening by a lengthening of the back (with domestic horses the usual number of dorsal vertebrae is eighteen).

Mongolian wild horses are born a bright yellow-brown, to which a mouse-grey shading soon gets added. But they lose their first, curly hair when they are a couple of weeks old and grow instead a smooth, summer-hair in colours characteristic of adult horses.

The colour of adult Mongolian wild horses ranges

between two extreme colour types. We should call one dun, whereas the other one is reminiscent of bay, though this latter is often paler, nearly sandy or grey. (These colours are termed kur and syr in Mongolian.) The external shape of the horses in these two colours is absolutely identical, and although Przevalsky horses of a dark ground colour are to be found most commonly in mountains and lighter ones on the steppe flatland, one cannot speak of two different geographical races on grounds of the colour only. The more so as dark- and light-coloured animals may occur in the same herd; and when dark mares are covered by dark stallions they often give birth to light foals, and vice versa. It also happens that with the passing of time a dark animal will grow paler in colour.

To whatever colour variant adult animals belong, their bellies are lighter and their heads (and sometimes their necks) are darker than the principal body colour. The part around the mouth is almost pure white, and a narrow white ring surrounds the eyes. At the same time the hairs on the rim of the ears are black, both inside and outside. The long hairs of the mane and tail are also dark and a black dorsal stripe follows the line of the spine, to end in the black hairs of the tail. Often a dark line crosses the shoulders, but it is never as sharp as that of asses. In very rare cases fox-red or yellow long hairs will also occur. These colours however do not point, in Mohr's opinion, to a presence of domestic horses' blood: she had herself observed it on pure-blood Przevalsky horses kept in zoos, whose pedigree had been recorded in stud-books. These animals had mostly quite light trunks.

Nor does she consider the star on the forehead, which here and there appears on individuals kept in zoos, the white or dark spots on the trunk, or dappled coats to be signs of the introduction of domestic horses' blood. She points out that piebald, white, yellow, albino, red, black or other exceptional individuals may occur in any species of wild animals living in free nature (bison, roe deer, hare, monkey, etc.), even when there are no domesticated forms.

However, the question is not quite so simple, particularly in the case of animals kept in a zoological garden. If white, piebald or dappled coats may appear as transformations due to domestication, captivity may also cause changes in animals. It would be advisable to examine the circumstances under which these animals are kept in captivity from this point of view, before coming to any firm conclusion.

The upper part of the legs is of a colour similar to that of the trunk. On the forelegs the dark stripes on the rear part of the forearm and the carpal are very interesting: they are common characteristics of primitive equids and occur among all groups of the *Equus* genus—wild horses, asses, half-asses and zebras—alike, but are quite exceptional among domestic horses. The distal parts of the extremities and the hooves are always black.

The Mongolian wild horse's mane and tail are quite conspicuous, neither of them being like those we usually see on domestic horses.

The mane is not long and overhangs sideways like that of domestic horses: it is short and erect. At its root it is broad and there the dark longer hairs of the mane are supported by shorter ones of the colour of the trunk. There is little if any forelock.

But, side by side with the typical form of the mane, a hanging mane also occurs now and then among Przevalsky horses, though it is never as long as the untrimmed one of domestic horses. This is simply due to the fact that the mane, having grown too long, hangs to the side. According to H. Heck's observation (1936) Przevalsky horses grow long manes if they are in poor condition, if they are old or if they are lonely. On the other hand Ewart (1909) noticed that some Przevalsky horses will grow long manes in spring.

No doubt long, overhanging manes on Przevalsky horses are connected with their age, their health and with whether or not they are well nourished. If an animal is ill or underfed, for instance, the muscles of the upper part of the neck get flaccid and do not hold the mane erect. As soon as the animal has regained its strength the mane will recover its original position. But manes are also affected, as Mohr observed, by any shift in the moulting time. It is not only the short hairs of the trunk that the Przevalsky horse sheds, as does the domestic horse, but also the dock hairs of the tail and those of the mane. If for some reason (illness, old age etc.), the spring moulting gets delayed, the mane will continue to grow and fall to the side by its very weight. This could be very well observed on Hamlet, the six-year-old Przevalsky stallion of Budapest Zoo. Its mane had always been absolutely regular, until 1970 when the long winter caused a delay in the spring moulting so that the horse's mane, thick with unevenly growing hair, fell to the left side of the neck.

At birth the foal of the Mongolian wild horse has no regular mane, there are only brush-like, separate, somewhat curly bunches of hair lined along the edge of its neck. The regular, erect mane gets developed rather late, when the foal is about half a year old.

The tail of the Przevalsky horse is somewhere between that of asses and half-asses, and that of the domestic horse. Asses' and half-asses' tails are like those of cattle: they have a tassel-like bunch of long hair at their end, whereas the dock is covered by short hair like that of the trunk. The tail of the domestic horse, on the other hand, is covered all along with long hair. On the two sides of the upper part of the Mongolian wild horse's dock there are hairs of the same colour as its coat. Between them there runs, on the back, a stripe of short hairs with the dorsal stripe in the middle. At the end of the dock it has long, dark hairs, such as those covering the whole of the domestic horse's tail.

Hairs on the upper part of the tail are shed like those on the coat; whereas the long ones, on the lower part, are not shed.

The whole question of moulting in the Mongolian wild horse is very interesting. Unlike in domestic horses and a number of other domestic and wild mammals, shedding takes place only once a year, as has been observed by V. Mazák. But new hairs grow twice annually. The changing of hairs begins at the end of March or the first half of April and lasts for one-and-a-half or two months. Then the animal grows short, straight hairs, and the hairs of the mane and tail are also completed. Instead of the autumn shedding usual with other animals, the Mongolian wild horse grows additional hairs in autumn. This begins between the middle of September and the first half of October and lasts two or two-and-a-half months. During that period thicker and longer hairs grow among those of the summer coat. These longer hairs are sometimes 10 cm long. The winter coat is usually of a lighter shade than the summer one; this is nothing but adjustment to the white colour of the snow-covered environment. In autumn winter hairs grow among the hairs of the mane too and thus the mane becomes not only longer but also thicker. The longest hairs of the mane, which are 14–16 cm in summer, are, on an average, 17–21 cm long in winter. With adult animals the change of the hairs of the mane follows about one and a half to three months after the change of the hairs of the trunk; with young animals the shedding and growing of new hairs of the mane and trunk take place at the same time. The winter hairs of the mane grow somewhat later than those of the other parts of the body. For winter, the animals grow a beard of coarse hair under their chin.

New and interesting programmes of research, aimed at throwing light upon new aspects of the Przevalsky horse, have been instituted into the chromosome patterns of the animal. Examinations at Catskill Game Farm of two pure-blooded Mongolian wild horses, whose origin was very well known, showed that the number of their chromosomes was not sixty-four as is usual with domestic horses, but sixty-six. These investigations—if they are confirmed by the results of further examinations of pure-blooded Przevalsky horses—may become extraordinarily important. Suffice it to imagine that the chromosome investigations may ascertain whether there is any domestic blood in a wild horse or not; moreover, these investigations may play a part in identifying the wild ancestors of different groups of domestic horses.

### ITS HABITAT, WAY OF LIFE

It does not seem to be useful to go into the question what the Przevalsky horses' habitat may have been like at the time when the subspecies evolved. Nevertheless, it is worth noting that even then their environment was probably more unfavourable than that in the chief distribution area of the species of wild horses in the Late Pleistocene and Early

Holocene periods; for it is thought that it was on account of the unfavourable environment that the Mongolian wild horse became diminished into a smaller edge-form.

Today Przevalsky horses have withdrawn, to escape man, to the salty steppe and the semi-desert. They cannot of course survive in the desert, for want of water. These territories are some 1,000–1,400 metres above sea-level, and the vegetation there is rather poor, consisting almost exclusively of salt-loving (halophilous) plants. There are no trees at all. Saxaul *(Haloxylon ammodendron)*, a shrub-like plant, grows tallest. Przevalsky wrote the following about this interesting plant: "*Haloxylon ammodendron* belongs to the salty plants. Its leafless branches look like tails and turn vertically upwards. The plant itself, called *zahk* by the Mongolians, looks like a crooked shrub or tree; it often grows as high as two fathoms. Near the roots the diameter of its trunk is fifteen to twenty-two cm. But it is very seldom that the *Haloxylon* grows as big as that, and this happens only in its favourite colonies, such as for example Ala-Shan, in the north, a *Haloxylon* paradise. It grows on the bare sand, mostly by itself. Side by side with the live plants there spread—or lie on the ground—the dead ones and therefore, if I may use this expression, a *Haloxylon* wood is not a very attractive sight, not even in the desert, for the wretched plant does not even offer shade. The soil on which it grows lacks any other plant and is so thoroughly harrowed by storms and gales that it is an endless alternation of ditches and hillocks.

"But to desert-dwellers the *Haloxylon* is worth its weight in gold, for it is good fodder for the camel and is excellent as fuel. Its wood is unusually heavy and hard and yet so fragile that at one strike of the axe even the biggest trunk breaks into splinters. . . . It blossoms in May. The tiny, yellow blooms are hardly noticeable. The seeds, too, are minute and flat; they are winged and grey; grow close to one another on the stem and ripen in September. . . ."

The *Salsola kali,* a small shrub-like, salty plant, whose small tufts can be practically the only vegetation of vast steppe lands, is also of great importance. The *Lasiagrostis splendens,* belonging to the Gramineae and called *dürisun* in Mongolian and *tchij* in Kirghizian, grows mostly around springs and wells. It grows into a small bush and reaches, in general, a height of 150–180 cm, but sometimes even 210–270 cm. Along with the saxaul it offers good hiding places for animals. In the Salsola steppe, however, a sizable animal is unable to hide.

Wormwood *(Artemisia incana)* also occurs in those parts, and so do feathergrass *(Stipa orientalis),* and a number of halophilous grasses. The wild horses' bill of fare is completed by the roots of rhubarb *(Rheum leucorhizum)* and by the bulbs of small tulips *(Tulipa uniflora).* In spring, this latter, blossoming in clumps on hillsides otherwise quite desolate, is a pleasant surprise for the traveller.

Recently Przevalsky horses seem to have been ousted even from the steppes and semi-deserts and to have withdrawn among the mountains. Thus it was that Kaszab observed them amidst practically impassable mountains at an altitude of about 2,000 metres above sea-level. Here the vegetation is even poorer, although it comprises essentially the same species as in the steppe and semi-desert.

Even today Mongolian wild horses cover excessive distances in the course of their wanderings. In summer they generally live in the plain of Djungharia and withdraw to the mountains of South-West Mongolia in winter; but lately there are indications that they—or at least groups of them—have not left the Mongolian mountains even in summer. To find food is the first reason for their roaming, but the fact that they are more sheltered in winter among the mountains than in the wind-swept steppe certainly also plays a role. Nor is the question of drinking water irrelevant. Przevalsky horses are rather modest in their requirements of water: they can do without it for two–three days and sometimes even for four, and they even drink salt water if it is not too concentrated. But they do have to adjust themselves to watering places. It is a well-known fact that South-West Mongolia is poor in water; in the area of Kobdo the annual precipitation is only about 100 metres? and even that falls in the form of snow. Indeed, from this point the situation of wild horses is easier in winter; but in summer, for want of any better solution, they cannot but dig with their fore-hooves a hole in spots situated rather low and drink the salt water accumulating in it.

The brothers Grum-Grshmailo gave a thorough report on the way of life of Przevalsky horses. Their description was published by Salensky in 1902:

"The wild horse is an inhabitant of the steppe flatland; it goes grazing and drinking at night. At sunrise it returns to the desert where it rests until sunset. In spring, when there are foals too in the group, the animals always take a rest at the same place. . . .

"Wild horses generally proceed in single file, particularly if they are fleeing some danger. Kulans and djiggetais, on the other hand, always crowd together when they are frightened and flee in complete confusion. Due to this custom of wild horses, namely that they advance in single file, one behind the other, there are deep runways stretching over the whole Gatchun region. . . .

"In case of danger the stallion runs forward only if there

57

are no foals in the group. If there are some, he will often run sideways and reveal with all his movements extraordinary anxiety; as against this the kulan is much more selfish and does not care about the danger threatening its harem and the young generation. . . .

"It was interesting to observe the stallion's behaviour. Scenting danger he snorted to warn the group; at once the horses lined up in single file with a young stallion in front, the foals keeping in the middle among the mares. As long as the group was moving the stallion remained on the side where the hunters were and directed the group either by the movements of his head or by the beats of his hooves to the course he had chosen. When the horses had broken through the ring of the hunters and the latter were chasing them quite nearby, the stallion took up a stand in the first battle line. It was funny to see how he goaded on a young foal, whose feeble legs were unable to keep it abreast with the others. Only when the foal began to fall behind did the mare, neighing softly, try to encourage it, but when she realized that this was of no use either, she got separated from the group for, obviously, she did not want to leave behind her young. But the stallion did not tolerate such disorderliness; with two powerful kicks he forced the mare to run after the group and took over the guarding of the foal himself."

Colonel Przevalsky himself pointed out how difficult it was to approach Mongolian wild horses—which is why there are so few observations on its way of life in free nature—and particularly to hunt and capture them. Other travellers have described in great detail the way in which such hunts are carried out: since wild horses live in steppes remote from all human habitation, a minor expedition has to be launched, which may last several weeks, and in the course of which the hunters may have to cover distances of hundreds of kilometres.

Winter is perhaps the best time for hunting, since then snow provides the hunters' water supply. For the hunt itself, horses—good runners—are needed first of all. We have seen in Kaszab's case that not even an overland car can overtake horses. Every hunter takes along a saddled led horse or two, and when during the chase one horse gets tired, he mounts the other one and leaves the tired animal back on the steppe. Whosoever has taken part in such a hunt emphasizes the heroism of the stallions, which defend their group to the death. As a rule only foals and young animals are captured, for trying to catch adults is a rather hopeless venture. The Mongolians' well-known lassos with sticks are used for capturing wild horses. The local nomadic horse-breeders are veritable virtuosi at handling the lasso: they have plenty of opportunity to practise on their own half-wild horses.

The wolf and the bear are the main natural enemies of the Mongolian wild horse. But the horse is more than a match for either of them: its formidable kicks will soon discourage even the strongest beast of prey from fighting against a stallion defending his group, or against mares anxious for their foals. It is interesting to note that whereas the mares always kick only backwards in the course of fighting, or with their hooves sprinkle their urine into the attacker's eyes, the stallions will bite and cut with their forelegs and only rarely use their hindlegs for kicking.

Thus man remains the greatest enemy of the Przevalsky horse in its natural environment. This has been particularly true since the spread of fire-arms. Though hunts were staged in bygone days by the nomadic peoples of Central Asia, not to procure meat but as warlike exercises or sport, these hunts did not result in killing too many horses. It was only after the introduction of modern rifles (essentially after the first world war) that hunting became a serious threat to the horses' survival.

In captivity too the Przevalsky stallion is an absolute lord of his group, which includes, apart from him, only mares, their foals and young stallions. The leading stallions demarcate the boundaries of their territories by their dung and urine, inspecting them regularly. If another stallion enters his domain, or even aproaches it, the stallion attacks immediately. It sometimes happens in zoos that a herd is joined by a mare who is not accustomed to the order the stallion has established, or does not want to accept it. First she is called to order by movements of the stallion's head; if this does not prove sufficient the stallion imposes his will by bites, then by gentler or stronger kicks.

The behaviour of Mongolian wild horses living in captivity is rather divergent. As a rule, they are all very timid at the beginning. Later they may grow braver, but they will never become particularly friendly. If lonely Przevalsky mares are enclosed in the same pen with other solidungulates they remain solitary and do not make friends with other animals; instead they rudely chase away any animal approaching them. However, perhaps because their maternal instincts survive, it has happened more than once that they have been seen to play with young asses or mules.

Mares, incidentally, will often fight among themselves, kicking away the foals of the others while jealously guarding their own. Stallions, on the other hand, do not play with their foals at all and treat them generally rather

60

coldly, as they treat the mares too, except in the mating period. Mostly it is the mares themselves who keep their foals apart from the stallion. In every group a leading mare follows the stallion in rank. In this "honour" mares will supersede one another from time to time.

The sequence in which food and water are taken is also significant. It is always the mares with foals that take precedence and only after they have fed do mares without foals or young animals take their turn. When they have finished, the stallion comes; but if it happens that he is impatient, he may chase the others away. When the stallion has drunk and begun to eat, the others can return.

Sometimes it happens even under circumstances prevailing in a zoo that two stallions come to fight. Seeing these fights one can imagine how savage such clashes can be in the Mongolian steppe. Often the fight starts without any particular preliminary sign, but at other times the stallions take up a so-called menacing posture. They lower their heads almost to the ground, lay back their ears and rush against each other. They chiefly bite, and kick viciously with their forelegs. They try to catch their opponents by the edge of the mane, throw them to the ground, and kill them by biting the nape of the neck or by striking them. Even if the keepers intervene in time the animals will frequently inflict serious injuries upon each other.

The mating time of Mongolian wild horses rather depends on the climate. In the Zoological Garden in Prague the mares come on heat, usually for two to four days, between May and July, and only exceptionally at other times. Covering is preceded by a long mating game and, generally, the stallion leaps upon the mare so passionately that, for a moment, his hind legs do not even touch the ground.

In the Prague Zoo it has been observed that mares

generally give birth to their foals from mid-April to mid-July. A few days before, the mare keeps aloof from other members of the group. After birth, which generally takes place at night or early in the morning, the mother carefully licks the whole body of her new-born foal to cleanse it thoroughly. Sometimes she eats up the foetal envelope. Meanwhile she closely guards her foal and tries to drive away any animal approaching it by shaking her head or, if this is not enough, by biting and kicking.

The Przevalsky foal has long legs and its rump is a bit overgrown. In the beginning it walks with difficulty because its joints are still a bit rigid. But within a few days it follows its mother everywhere and ventures upon independent excursions within a diameter of twenty–thirty inches. Of course, its mother will keep an eye on it all the time, so that she may rush to its protection as soon as needed. When it is two or three days old it starts playing; at first only with its mother but from the time it is a week old it will play with other foals too.

At three to five years the Przevalsky mare is ripe for mating, and some continue to bear progeny even after their twentieth year of age. It is somewhat later that stallions are able to cover successfully, and stallion Sidney 5, No 226, of the Zoological Garden of Sidney, was still fertile at the age of twenty-six. The greatest age known to have been reached by a Przevalsky horse is that of a mare who died at the age of thirty-four; and in 1959 there was a stallion in the twenty-eighth year of his life still alive.

Bubenik (1961) made some fascinating observations of the daily life rhythm of Mongolian wild horses in the Zoo in Prague. He found that behaviour was intimately connected with the animal's position in the group and with its age. It is, first and foremost, to the leading stallion of the group that the members of the group adjust themselves; his burdens, both psychical and physiological, are very great indeed. Following him in rank are the leading mares of the subgroups within the group.

He also found that wild horses are exceedingly sensitive to nervous stress and that in response to a stimulus a typical form of behaviour may easily turn into an atypical one. Degrees of sensitivity to stress again depend on the animal's rank in the herd and on its age.

## THE PRZEVALSKY HORSE IN HISTORIC SOURCES
## AND IN MONGOLIAN FOLKLORE

Ever since prehistoric times the Mongolian wild horse, as a characteristic member of the mammal fauna of Central Asia, must have attracted the attention of a great many people. So it is strange that it is extraordinarily seldom mentioned in literature.

If we compare it, for example, with its relative, the Mongolian half-ass, the kulan, then we find that in Mediaeval sources there are no less than fifty references to the kulan for every one to the Przevalsky horse. Thus in the famous *Secret History of the Mongolians* the wild horse is mentioned a single time; nor was it mentioned at all in the reports of European envoys sent to the Mongolian court, or by missionaries, in spite of the fact that their reports often dealt with the smallest details. It seems likely that this reticence was due not only to the fact that Mongolian wild horses were much rarer than kulans, but also to the extreme timidity of the horses, and their peculiarly secretive way of life. This in turn was no doubt the consequence of man having hunted the wild horse much more than the kulan, for he could not domesticate the latter and killed it only for its flesh, whereas the former was useful also because foals captured alive increased men's herds.

1 Colonel N. M. Przevalsky (1839–1888), who discovered the Mongolian wild horse. This picture, now published for the first time, was taken before he set out on his second tour of Central Asia. From the collection of the Zoological Institute of the Soviet Academy of Sciences, Leningrad.

2 Group of Mongolian wild horses encountered by Z. Kaszab in the Takhiyn Shara-nuru Mountains in 1966. Photo Kaszab.

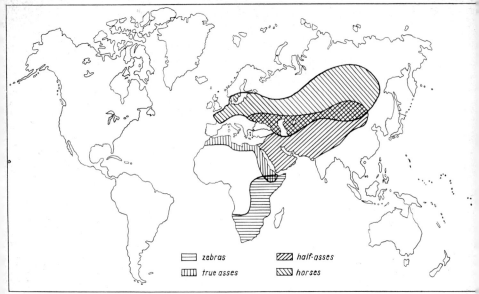

zebras ▭     half-asses ▨

true asses ▥     horses ◿

3   Distribution area of the equids' subgenera in the early Holocene. As can be seen, the distribution areas partly overlap. Individuals of the subgenera do not however cross-breed in the wild.

4   Representation of a Przevalsky horse from a silver vase from Maikop (Kuban region), ca. 2200 B.C. After Frankfort (1954).

5   Rock drawings of wild horses from Shishkino, from the region of the sources of the River Lena. Upper Paleolithic. Though the horses are not easy to identify, they can only be Przevalsky horses or their direct predecessors, considering the period and the geographic situation.

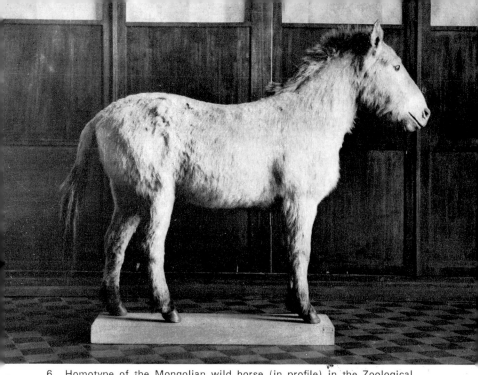

6   Homotype of the Mongolian wild horse (in profile) in the Zoological Institute of the Soviet Academy of Sciences in Leningrad. Collected by Colonel Przevalsky.

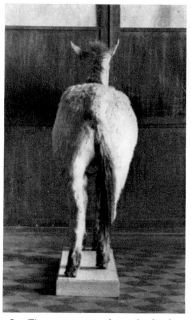

7   The same, seen from the front.          8   The same, seen from the back.

9  Drawing of a Mongolian wild horse in Przevalsky's book. It was probably made by I. V. Roborovsky, a member of Przevalsky's expedition, who later continued the Colonel's exploratory work. Though the drawing presents numerous characteristic features of the Mongolian wild horse it delineates the legs in a way similar to those of noble domestic ones: exaggerating the shortness of the dockhairs, it shows the tail almost as if it were that of an ass.

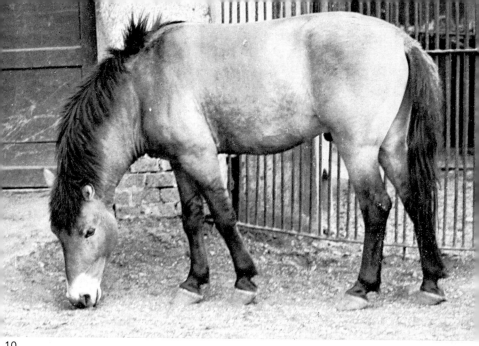

10

1

12

13

**10, 11, 12, 13 & 14**

*Top:* On account of the long winter the shedding of hairs was protracted and the mane grew too long. The horizontal stripes above the hocks of the forelegs are clearly discernible.

*Above left:* The massive neck and the whitish colour around the mouth. The mane, grown too long because of the long winter, hangs to the forehead.

*Above centre:* Hamlet.

*Above right:* The hairs on the dock are short, and the dorsal stripe extends to the tail.

*Left:* Horizontal stripes on the forelegs of the six-year-old Mongolian wild stallion Hamlet. Photos Konya

14

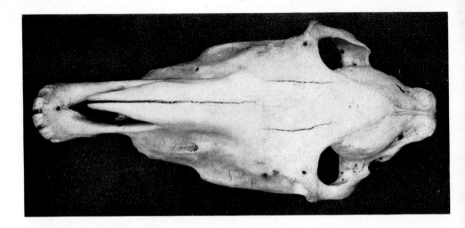

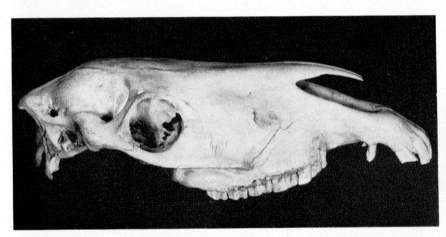

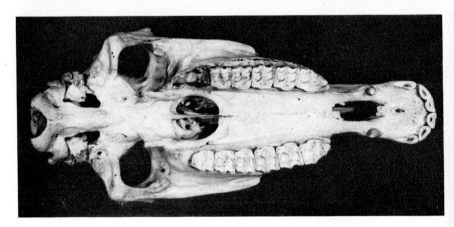

15, 16 & 17 Skull of Przevalsky stallion. Martin Duther Universität,
Julius Kühn Collection, Halle/Saale. Photo Londner.

18  Mongolian wild horses playing at Askania Nova. Photo Anghi.

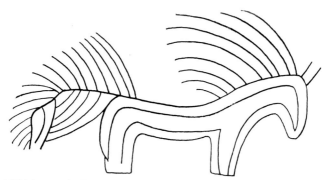

19  Wild horse. Incised decoration of a Tartar wooden bucket from the
Altai. After Ivanov.

20 Tarpan. From the mural of the Sophia Church in Kiev. After Heptner.

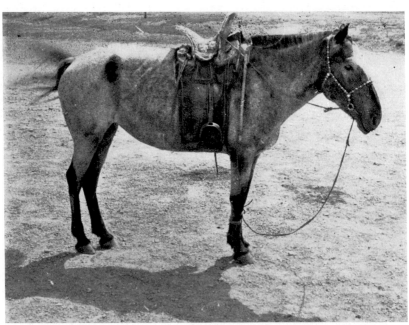

21 Mongolian domestic horse, whose skull is strongly reminiscent of Mongolian wild horses, with silver studded bridle and saddle. Photo Erdélyi.

22   Mongolian horsemen, one of them with a lasso with stick. Photo Teichert.

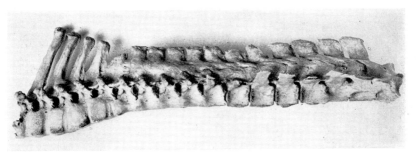

23   The dorsal and lumbar vertebrae, grown together, of the horse from the Avar tomb at Keszthely. In profile. Photo Karát.

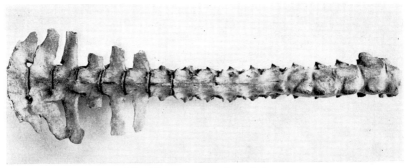

24   The same seen from below.

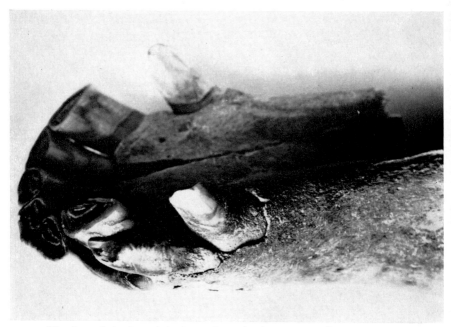

25 Part of the jaw of the horse from the Avar tomb at Keszthely. Beside the third left incisor and in front of the canine tooth a supernumerary tooth is clearly visible. Photo Karát.

26 Przevalsky foal that died soon after its arrival, from the second Hagenbeck consignment. Naturkunde Museum, Stuttgart.

27 Orlitza III-Mongol, the only Przevalsky mare born in the wild and living in Europe, with her two foals in Askania Nova. Photo Anghi.

28 Group of Mongolian wild horses in Askania Nova. Photo Anghi.

29 Mongolian wild horses in their winter coat in the animal park of Hellabrunn. The long, shaggy hair and the "beard" below the chin can be clearly observed. Photo Angermayer.

30 Sars (Askania III), a stallion, one of the sons of Orlitza III-Mongol, in his winter coat in Prague Zoo in December 1968. Photo J. Volf.

31  Verita (Praha 79), the Przevalsky mare born in July 1966 in Prague Zoo and transferred to Aalborg in 1969. Photo J. Volf, December 1968.

32  Przevalsky foal in Prague Zoo. Photo J. Volf.

33 Przevalsky stallion in San Diego Zoo, a characteristic example of the light colour variant. The upper third of its tail is covered with short hairs only. The white colouring around the muzzle can also be seen. Photo Bökönyi.

34 Mongolian wild stallion born in free nature, then kept in Talbolug, Mongolia, where it died about 1959. Several hybrids that he sired with Mongolian domestic mares are still alive. Probably this was the wild horse Dr. C. Purkyne mentioned. Photo Tshevegmid.

35 Przevalsky mares at Shargantului, on the model farm for educational purposes at the Academy of Agriculture of Ulan Bator. Both of them were born in the wild and brought to the model farm in 1944. Their further fate is unknown. Photo Purkyne, after Mohr.

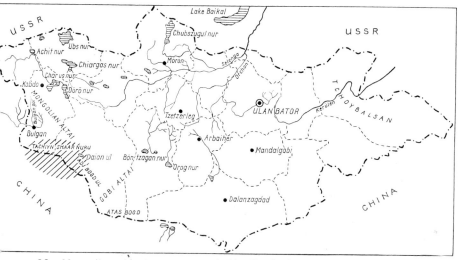

36 Mongolia, with the present probable distribution area (hatched part) of the Przevalsky horse.

37 The Takhin Shara-nuru Mountains, the last area to which Mongolian wild horses have withdrawn. Photo Kaszab.

38 Characteristic habitat of the Mongolian wild horse in the Takhin Shara-nuru Mountains. Photo Kaszab.

As a parallel the case of the bison and of the aurochs can be mentioned. The bison, which cannot be domesticated, escaped extinction and is alive even today, though the killing of a bison supplied a huge quantity of meat. On the other hand the aurochs, the wild ancestor of our domestic cattle, became extinct around the turn of the first millennium A.D. in the greater part of Europe, and did not survive even in territories hardly ever invaded by man, such as the vast forests of Poland.

The last century's accounts of travels by European travellers, who were the first to penetrate Mongolia and its surroundings, reflect the same proportion between the kulan and the wild horse. In Przevalsky's travel book, for example, kulans are mentioned innumerable times, for he had seen them in herds of hundreds, and only met wild horses twice. In the course of his travels his pupil, P. K. Koslov, also met kulans several times, and wild horses only once; nor did the rest of the explorers of Central Asia fare better.

One work in which wild horses are mentioned is a book dating back to the first half of the eleventh century entitled *Precious Tales* by the Tibetan author Bodo.

The other early reference is in the already mentioned *Secret History of the Mongolians,* which tells how in the Year of the Dog (1226) Genghis Khan set out on his campaign against Tangut. ". . . on the way (he) staged a hunt against the mass of wild horses of Arbuka: Genghis Khan was riding the Sorrel Roan. Suddenly wild horses ran across his path in front of him, the Sorrel Roan reared and Genghis Khan fell from the horse to the ground." Tangut comprised the area west from the great bend of the Yellow River up to the Ecin Gol, including Ordos, a part of the Shensi and Khansu provinces, and Ninghia. Genghis Khan's hunt probably took place north of this territory.

The notes of the Chancellor of Tchetchen Khan are of a much later date, in 1637. According to them the Khan ordered a wild horse to be captured in the area of the Takhiyn-nus and presented it to the Emperor of Manchuria.

Although all this is rather meagre information, it proves at least one important fact: namely that the wild horse must have been highly appreciated, princely game in the seventeenth century. What could otherwise have been the explanation for its being given as a present to the Emperor of Manchuria?

In Mongolian folklore the wild horse appears somewhat more frequently. Here too it is deemed a noble animal, often the symbol of the love of freedom, which will perish rather than endure captivity: allusion to the fact that an adult animal cannot be domesticated.

In Mongolian folk-poetry the wild horse is always the embodiment of strength, of vehemence and of power. Heroes and khans are compared to the wild horse. In one epic, for instance, Djangrai Khan laughs in a voice as roaring as that of the tiger and as sharp as that of the takhi.

The wild horse often occurs in the Mongolians' songs praising the horse and in their sacrificial chants to accompany libations. Thus in a sacrificial chant for a load-bearing strap the person performing the sacrificial rite begs for a successful hunt and for killing the takhi, the kulan and the fat-breasted maral deer.

Local place-names too make frequent use of the name of the Mongolian wild horse. A good example of this is the sandy steppe Takhiyn-nus (Wild Horse Brook) in the north-eastern part of Central Mongolia where, in the seventeenth century, the wild horse for the Emperor of Manchuria was caught. Although wild horses have not occurred there for

66

long, the name has persistently survived. Another name of this kind is the sacrificial mound Takhi-yin sangda-u quddug-un-obog-a, that is to say, the mound at the well (watering place) of the wild horse. This one too originates from times when wild horses were more often to be seen, perhaps because they were not so much disturbed by the appearance of man. The sacrificial mound, called obo, was raised along a roadway, every passer-by placing some object on it and thus further increasing it.

Representations of wild horses also appear now and then in Mongolia and in other regions of the Altai. Images are often found incised on tombstones, although sometimes in forms rather difficult to recognize; and drawings or carvings representing wild horses may decorate objects of everyday use. These are often very beautiful, and it is a pity that wooden objects are not very durable and so we can know only the more recent representations. Perhaps the most beautiful among them is a drawing on a Tartar wooden bucket of the Altai. It represents, in a very interesting artistic approach, a thickset wild horse with an erect mane. The tail is of the structure of a feather, the hairs being placed on the dock like branches on the quill of a feather. Though wild horses have not particularly bushy tails the folk-artist may have wanted to indicate in this way the tail ruffled by the wind.

# THE PRZEVALSKY HORSE AND EUROPEAN WILD HORSES

It is evident from Nobis' analysis that a uniform Eurasian group of wild horses, medium or small in size, had come into being by the end of the Pleistocene. It survived the drastic changes of the climate at the end of the Ice Age and survived into the Neolithic.

However, it was not in all parts of Europe that the wild horses survived the end of the Pleistocene. Whereas in Southern Sweden, in Switzerland, Germany, Russia and the Ukraine great numbers of remains were discovered in practically all sites of the Early Holocene, and recently even in the Neolithic sites of the Baltic, horses are completely missing from Early Holocene sites of other regions of the European continent. Thus for example, not a single piece of authentic remains of horses from the period between approximately 7,000 and 3,000 B.C. has been found in the Basin of the Carpathians or in the Balkans. (The period by and large corresponds with the whole of the Neolithic period and, in certain places, includes the beginning of the Copper Age as well). Only in a domesticated form did horses find their way to these territories: in small numbers in the course of the Copper Age, and in great masses at the beginning of the Bronze Age.

Nor did wild horses survive for very long in the western part of Europe. The area was soon populated, the extent of cultivated land grew by leaps and bounds; livestock-keeping and animal domestication at the end of the Neolithic and the beginning of the Bronze Age soon reduced the number of wild horses. To escape man they withdrew to forests and mountains, but they were not left in peace there either, for man hunted them. It seems likely that these wild horses did not survive even into the Middle Ages, and that those sometimes mentioned in Mediaeval sources were only feral domestic ones.

But in the eastern part of Europe—essentially in territories east of the Oder—there were wild horses in great numbers in the Early Holocene. In some Neolithic sites of the Ukraine they were found to have been the animal most hunted, indicating that Neolithic man did not turn up his nose at horse-flesh. Since at that time there were not yet any domestic horses, wild horses could not be hunted on horseback, but they were evidently caught by traps, or perhaps in corrals. In this latter case entire hordes, or maybe even several hordes, had to join forces to drive the herd of wild horses into an already-prepared corral.

In the woodland zone of Eastern Europe the number of wild horses may have been smaller. Here their northern-most occurrence may have been the southern coastal district of the Baltic Sea, where Paaver found bones of horses in the hunting spoils of one Neolithic settlement in the south of Latvia and in one of Southern Estonia.

Wild horses occurred in later periods too in Eastern Europe, but it is very difficult to tell their bones from those of domestic horses. On the other hand, from the Middle Ages onwards written sources do make mention of them.

Thus Albertus Magnus (1193–1280) wrote about the wild horses of Prussia, describing them as ash-coloured (cinereus), with a dark dorsal stripe. S. von Heberstein, who travelled to Lithuania in 1517 and in 1528, and recorded his experiences in writing in 1549, also reported on wild horses. According to him they were cream-coloured, which corresponds with the ash-grey described by Albertus Magnus. Lithuanian wild horses became extinct towards the end of the eighteenth century, more or less at the same time, or somewhat earlier than, those of Poland.

It was in the Ukraine that European wild horses survived longest. The Greek historian Herodotus mentioned them in book four of his work, when describing the Scythians' country: ". . . the Hypanis (the present River Bug) comes from Scythia and springs from a great lake around which white wild horses are grazing." These horses, the tarpans, so often debated in the literature of zoology (tarpan or turpan is a Turkoman word and sounds almost identically in Bashkirian, in Kazakh and in Tartar), were first described by Gmelin, the well-known traveller. He rallied peasants around him and staged a hunt after the tarpan. They killed a stallion and two mares and captured a foal. At the same time he made close observations and it is to him that we owe the best description of the tarpan.

According to this description the tarpan is of the same size as the smallest Russian domestic horse. Its head is massive, the ears being pointed and sometimes rather long. The eyes are fiery, the mane is short and erect. Its tail is more or less (?) covered with hair and is shorter than that of domestic horses. The tarpan's colour is mouse-grey (though mention is made of white and ash-grey individuals seen elsewhere), its belly is ash-grey, the legs are black downwards from their middle. The hair is very long and thick, so much so that one would rather think of a fur than of a horse's fell.

The tarpans live in small groups, each under the leadership of one stallion. The stallions often abduct domestic mares and Gmelin himself saw such a mare in the group he was chasing. The stallions are unbelievably strong; they seek fights with domestic stallions and vanquish them.

This description of the tarpan was completed later by the Pole Vetulani, an outstanding scientist of East-European archaic breeds of horses. He pursued experiments in reconstituting the wild tarpan and with a view to this settled Polish *konik* horses, whose exterior is appropriate, in the forests of Bialoviezha. It could be observed on these horses that in the course of the autumn shedding they grew chiefly white hairs. This was the organism's spontaneous camouflage, to make the body melt into the white environment. Bearing this in mind, Herodotus' description of white wild horses at once becomes comprehensible; they were evidently tarpans in their winter coat, as were the white and ash-coloured individuals described by Gmelin too.

This whitening in winter is quite common not only with Polish koniks but with Carpathian *hutsul* horses as well. I knew myself several individuals of this archaic breed, whose trunk became in winter several shades lighter, whereas the covering hairs of the head and of the distal parts of the extremities and, needless to say, the hairs of the mane and the tail remained black.

According to the Russian zoologist Heptner the last tarpan—which however lived in captivity and not in free nature—perished only in 1918–19. It was a stallion of 140–145 cm withers height, with a big head, a broad forehead and a straight profile. His ears were small and pointed, his

71

neck was short and so was the straight back, while the rump was sway-backed. He was mouse-grey with a dorsal stripe about two cm wide running along the middle of the back and with a blurred stripe across the shoulders. His mane was very short, strikingly thick and erect. This animal used to live in the surroundings of Poltava, together with a group of Kirghizian mares. He was very savage and would often attack the carriages of people travelling in the steppe. He would tear the harnesses off the mares and abduct them. He sired several foals with the mares of his harem and these foals looked definitely like wild horses, only their manes were somewhat longer than that of their sire.

On the basis of the two tarpan skulls, one complete with the skeleton in the Zoological Institute in Leningrad and the other in the Institute for Evolution History in Moscow —this is all that is extant of the East-European wild horse —the above description could be completed by the observation that in its entirety the skull was broad and spacious, with orbits rising above the plane of the forehead and with a markedly short facial part.

In the steppes of South Russia and the Southern Ukraine, to which they had withdrawn to escape man, the tarpans fared very well. However, after the Russian-Turkish wars the Turks were forced out of these territories and animal keepers began to populate the steppes. Soon these people had trouble with the wild horses. Not only did they pilfer their winter reserves of hay (the peasants told Gmelin that a group of tarpans was able to eat up a whole haystack in one night), but the tarpan stallions also carried away domestic mares. Soon an organized campaign was launched to exterminate the tarpans and their numbers soon began to decrease. In the early 'seventies of the last century a group would appear here and there, but later only a few individuals escaped the slaughter. Finally only a single mare survived, who joined herds kept in the steppe and twice gave birth to foals sired by domestic stallions. This mare lived not a long way from Falz-Fein's estate at Askania Nova, the place to which the first imported Przevalsky foals found their way.

In the winter of 1879 the peasants and smallholders of the region organized a hunt against this mare. In the following I quote a description by a participant in the hunt, taken from Falz-Fein's writings.

"The peasants of Agaimany and some small-holders of the region, who had heard that the mare had made an appearance, staged a hunt, or rather a persecution of the horse. Riders, mounted on the best horses of the area, rallied. Mounted vanguards were posted at great distances from one another and the mare was chased towards the first of these vanguards. This latter took up the hunt towards the second and that one towards the third, etc. On the day of the hunt the terrain was covered with a fairly thick coat of snow, the surface of which had been frozen to hard ice. Tempestuous blizzard aggravated the situation. In spite of all this the animal surmounted all obstacles with fabulous ease and would never have been caught if it had not broken one of its forelegs at a jump when one of its hooves got stuck in a crevice. It was laid on a sledge and taken to Agaimany, where it was admired by the whole population. They tried to cure it and had the village barber make an artificial hoof for it but after a few days it died."

However, in the Zaporozhye region or in the steppes of Tauria a group of tarpans seems to have survived for a time and it may have been the last members of that group, mentioned by Heptner, that got to the region of Poltava. But it is not very likely that these last tarpans were pure-blood wild horses. The stallion mentioned by Heptner, for instance, was relatively big and its short mane, falling to both sides, covered about two thirds of its neck.

Two essential questions arise in connection with the tarpan: first, is the tarpan a real wild horse or only a feral domestic one? And second, what is its relationship to the Przevalsky horse? Is it an independent species or do the two horses—as subspecies—belong to a single species? As we are going to see, the two questions are closely linked.

The first question is significant today only from the point of view of the history of science. It was first asked at the end of the last century or the beginning of this when researchers had already only descriptions of the tarpan and the two extant tarpan skulls to work with. Soon two camps came into being: one maintaining that the tarpan was an original wild horse, the other that it was a feral domestic one. This debate continued—without advancing from the field of theoretical considerations—up to the period right before the second world war.

A decisive development took place in the 'fifties and 'sixties. By then archaeological excavations had brought to light a great quantity of subfossil remains of wild horses, the investigation of which has proved that in East Europe the wild horses of the end of the Ice Age and the tarpans of the last century were connected by an unbroken chain of generations. Thus the whole prehistory of the tarpan became illuminated and even the most fervent opponents of the wild origin theory could not but give in. The few recalcitrants could do no more than insist that the tarpan described by Falz-Fein was a feral domestic horse, or a bastard of domestic and wild horse (though neither this nor its opposite could be proved), or that the two extant tarpan skulls had originated from such animals.

To answer the second question is more difficult. No doubt, there are several differences between the tarpan and the Mongolian wild horse both in form and colouring. First of all, the tarpan is somewhat smaller than and not so massive as the Mongolian wild horse. Its head is smaller too, the muzzle part shorter and the forehead definitely broad. (It was indeed on grounds of these two latter features that several hippologists considered the last tarpans to be domestic horses or cross-breds. But this view is contradicted by the fact that numerous proofs of the existence of wild horses with short muzzles and broad heads of the Ice Age—a period when there could be no domestic horses at all—have been found). East-European wild horses are mouse-grey, a colour that but exceptionally occurs with Mongolian wild horses. Moreover the whitening of the coat in winter, characteristic of the tarpan, appears on Mongolian wild horses only in that their coats become a little paler in winter.

The question next arises as to whether those differences are sufficient for considering two independent species of wild horses in the tarpan and in the Przevalsky horse. According to the taxonomy of animals based on morphology, which used to prevail, these differences would seem to be enough. Thus Antonius described the tarpan in 1912 as an independent species, the *Equus gmelini*, in the honour of Gmelin, the first to mention it. Sokolov's opinion (1967) was more or less the same. He wrote the following of the two wild horses:

"It is a case of two wild horse populations of very close origins; they discontinued free cross-breeding between each other in their natural habitat due to geographical, physiological or other reasons. Animals that owing to divergent evolutions independent of each other evolved real morphological differences should, in my view, be classified into different species. Probably this is the case with the tarpan and the Przevalsky horse. . . ."

But modern systematics, based on biology, which regards a species as a natural mating community, is of a different opinion. This view, basing its opinion on the fact—evinced by excavated finds—that the wild horses of Europe and Asia belonged to a population that lived in a contiguous territory at the end of the Pleistocene and the beginning of the Holocene—ranks them as a single species. Heptner, for example, has summarized all such wild horses as one single species under the name of tarpan, but has denominated them—rather confusingly—as *Equus przewalskii.* Within this species he recognizes three subspecies: the steppe tarpan (*Equus przewalskii gmelini,* which is the wild horse of South Russia), the forest tarpan (*Equus przewalskii sylvaticus,* which lived in the northern part of East Europe and in territories west of it), and the Djungharian or eastern tarpan (*Equus przewalskii przewalskii,* which is nothing else than the Mongolian wild horse). Nobis, too, classified (1970) the wild horse of East Europe into the same species as the Mongolian wild horse. He—as already mentioned—denominated it *Equus ferus,* this being the oldest of such names. However, as against Heptner, he did not consider the forest tarpan an independent subspecies, only a representative of the edge-form, which had got smaller.

# THE PRZEVALSKY HORSE AND THE ORIGIN
## OF THE DOMESTIC HORSE

Among our domestic animals the horse takes a special rank, being the species that has got closest to man. In this respect it has been surpassed only by the dog, though only in developed countries and in recent times. Franck, the great German hippologist, was right when he declared: "To write the history of the horse is really tantamount to writing the history of mankind."

And, indeed, although the horse does not belong to our most ancient domestic animals, for in Eurasia, for instance, it had been preceded by five species of Neolithic domestic animals—cattle, sheep, pigs and dogs—it acquired a stupendous significance right after its domestication. As a draught-animal it revolutionized transport and hence commerce too. True, it was not the first species to be used as a draught-animal for it had been preceded by cattle; but for speed the horse was without a rival. Because of this speed it was suited to long distance transport; and once goods could be conveyed quickly over great distances, commerce developed by leaps and bounds.

The horse had a similarly revolutionary effect upon warfare. Here too it was at first used chiefly as a draught-animal, and only in time emerged as a saddle animal. This is quite natural if we consider that the earliest attempts at domestication of equids had been in the Near East, with half-asses, much smaller and weaker than horses. Half-asses would hardly have been able to bear a rider's weight and it would have been particularly difficult for them to trot or gallop with a rider on their back. So they were harnessed into two-wheeled chariots. These attempts at domestication finally proved to be unsuccessful, for captured and tamed onagers did not breed in captivity (if animals do not breed in captivity, we can speak only of taming and not of domestication). Nevertheless, they were a success from one point of view at least: they brought into being the use of chariots in wartime, a practice which later, when horses had been domesticated, became fully effective. Soon afterwards cavalry came into being and the application of these two branches of military service had an impact on warfare the significance of which can be compared only with that of the tank in the first World War. By the time the first mounted nomadic armies had swept in wave upon wave over Europe from the early Iron Age onwards, the horse's role in shaping history was clear.

When and where did man first capture wild horses and make them his domestic animals? This too is a difficult question, first of all because the changes evolving in consequence of domestication were not so great in horses as they were with other species of domestic animals. If bones of cattle, sheep, goats, pigs or even dogs are unearthed at some prehistoric site it is fairly easy, in most cases, to ascertain whether they originated from the wild or from the domesticated form of the species. With these species domestication caused morphological changes (the body becoming smaller, the skull shorter and broader, the horns smaller, the dentition and the proportion of the bones of the limbs transformed) which are relatively easy to recognize. Quite different, however, is the case of the horse. True, with this species too the body became a bit smaller, but this took a long time. And in the skull the changes caused by domestication are minimal. The decrease in capacity of the brain case, the broadening of the forehead, the shortening of the facial part and the narrowing of the muzzle can be included among these changes. As a result of domestication the teeth also became smaller, but the irregular position of the teeth (e.g. growing crosswise in their row, or crowded together echelon-like), so frequent with pigs and dogs, does not occur with horses.

Of course, there are changes, indubitably evincing domestication, in the horse too. However, these do not appear in the skeleton but in decaying parts of the body: piebaldness, a hanging mane and forelock, marks on the forehead, lack of pigment in the distal parts of the extremities etc., all transformations that cannot be deduced from excavated remains but only from representations, which are very rare. Other changes that appeared very late are either dwarfing, or extreme growth in size.

Thus we cannot but try to find a method which enables us to establish in an indirect way the domestication of the horse in the material found in prehistoric sites. It is evident, for instance, that the presence of domestic horses might be revealed by pieces of harness found on the sites. This is how the saying, so very often quoted, of the German archaeologist G. Hermes was born: "Wo die Trense, dort ist in der Regel auch das gezähmte Pferd. . . ." (Where the bit is, there, as a rule, is the tamed horse too. . . .) In this connection, however, the problem arises that the first pieces of harness seemed to have been made entirely of materials (leather, yarns or tendons) that have disintegrated

79

in the earth: they had no parts made of metal or bone. In areas where wild horses did not survive the end of the Pleistocene and to which domesticated horses found their way again, parts of harness were not found for a long time. The first bits made of antlers or bone were produced at least a thousand years later than horses had first been domesticated, and bridles made of bronze appeared much later still.

The problem has been approached from quite a different aspect by the Soviet Artsikhovskij. In his opinion the presence of very old animals, an approximately identical number of mares and stallions, and a lack of vertebrae and breast-bones points to a wild population; whereas a lack of old animals, an overwhelming majority of mares and the occurrence of complete skeletons evince a domesticated stock.

No doubt, this is an ingenious argument, for it takes into consideration not only the shift of age and gender groups, which was the result of domestication, and the fact that in the refuse pits of a settlement other bones of animals kept in the settlement can be found than in the case of animals hunted and killed perhaps at quite a distance from the settlement. Obviously the primitive hunter, having killed a large beast a long way from the settlement, would not drag along the whole carcass but only the parts with plenty of flesh, leaving those with but little flesh on them on the spot of the killing. At the same time, when an animal kept on the settlement was killed and consumed, all of its bones were thrown into the refuse pit, with the exception of such as may have been taken away by dogs.

On the other hand, this method has the shortcoming that, with the exception of some settlements in the south of the Ukraine, there is not a single Early Holocene site in the whole of Europe where a sufficient number of horse bones to be perfectly adequate for the purposes of such an examination could be found. However, if, by way of completing the picture, we take into consideration the variation of the dentition and of the size of the body (since domestication increases the number of variations), we can ascertain with a fair percentage of probability whether we are confronted with domestic horses or wild ones.

For a long time we could rely only on theories and on guesswork with respect to the place where horses had been domesticated first. Quite a number of early domestication centres were supposed to have existed: Central Asia and South Russia being those most often mentioned. Anyhow, two things seemed to be doubtless: first of all that the southern part of Europe could by no means be taken into consideration, since there wild horses did not survive the end of the Ice Age. Secondly, it was evident that domestication had to take place earliest in an area where the optimal conditions of living for the species obtained. As early as 1963 I wrote the following:

"The earliest and most significant domestication of horses may have occurred in the steppe lands of Asia or of East Europe, for it was only there that a population of great numbers of wild horses surviving the Pleistocene could be found in the Neolithic period. As a result of the first introduction of domesticated horses from there to Europe domestication was commenced in this latter region too. This however—at least in the greater part of Central Europe—was never done on a major scale there; it was always horses introduced from the east that played a predominant role."

81

And, indeed, this was so. Recently (1967) the Ukrainian zoologist V. I. Bibikova found in the south of the Ukraine a centre of horse domestication, the earliest according to our present state of knowledge. In the Neolithic sites of the south of the Ukraine bones of horses were generally very frequent, indicating that in the steppe of the region wild horses lived in great masses under very good conditions. In the Eneolithic site (approximately the second half of the fourth millennium B.C.) at Dereivka on the right bank of the Dnieper, about 70 km from the town of Krementchug, there were extraordinarily large numbers of horse bones found: about 60 per cent (2,225 pieces) of the 3,703 bones of mammals that could be identified on the site. Even if this huge number of horse bones had originated from hunts, this very point may have raised the suspicion of domestication; for, according to observations made in Neolithic sites in Hungary, the domestication of cattle had always been linked with large-scale hunts of the aurochs. But a complete skull, which surely originated from a domestic horse, was also found, and certain bones of the extremities too pointed to domestication.

Thus the Southern Ukraine was the first centre in Europe for the domestication of horses, and it was from there that domestic horses soon spread. At first one by one, and then, from the beginning of the Bronze Age, that is about 2,000 B.C. onwards, in great numbers they spread out to other parts of Europe. Realizing the usefulness of the introduced domestic horse, man started the domestication of local wild horses in certain regions of Central and Western Europe too, though this process was never so significant as in the region of the earliest domestication.

We know far less about the centre of domestication in

Asia. In proportion to the vast territory of Siberia and Central Asia only a very few sites have been excavated, and although recently archaeological work has advanced by leaps and bounds, we have practically no data about the initial stages of horse-keeping. That is why many authors have argued that Asian wild horses were never domesticated at all.

Although there are but few archaeological proofs at our disposal, on grounds of biological considerations we must nevertheless assume that at least one Asian centre where horses were domesticated existed. It must have been somewhere in the steppes of Siberia or in Turkistan. It is not probable that early domestication took place in the present distribution area of Przevalsky horses, since this on the contrary is the region to which the last wild horses of Asia withdrew in response to threat of capture and domestication.

Cheng-Te-Kun published some very interesting data in 1959, indicating that the inhabitants of Lin-hai probably kept horses, side by side with dogs, sheep and cattle, in 4,000–3,000 B.C. Unfortunately, we do not know on what grounds he considered the horses found there to be domestic ones. Should these horses really have been domestic animals, they could either have been the products of local domestication only (nowhere else in Central Asia has evidence of domestication of horses at an earlier date been found); or, on the other hand, evidence that the domestication of horses in Central Asia may have been coeval with the earliest domestication in Europe. This is very easily conceivable. It could have been as a result of such domestication that the Proto-Turkic culture of horse-breeding came into being in North-China, north of the line Mukden, Peking, Haiphong, Shianphu, Lanchow, Shinning,

83

Karashar. This territory is adjacent to the eastern border of the former distribution area of Przevalsky horses, thus it may well be assumed that Przevalsky horses were themselves domesticated.

As against this the finds of horses' remains originating from the steppe region and the wooded steppes of Northern Asia (Afanasyevo culture, the region of Minusinsk) and of the Trans-Baikal territory (Eneolithic, 2,000–1,700 B.C.), are relatively late. Although we know for certain that these are remains of domestic horses, for they were identified by Vera Gromova, perhaps the best Soviet specialist of ancient horses' remains, it is not so certain that they originated from the domestication of local wild horses, since by then great numbers of domestic horses may have found their way to the area. Nevertheless, the possibility of local domestication cannot be excluded.

Researchers contesting the idea that Mongolian wild horses were domesticated, have asserted as a counter-argument first of all the circumstance that Mongolian and other Asian horses had short muzzles and broad heads and that the structure of their skull was reminiscent of that of the tarpan, and thus quite unlike that of the typical domestic horse in Asia. But, apart from the fact that domestication shortens the skull and broadens the forehead, and thus the skull of domesticated Przevalsky horses will not be an exact replica of that of original wild horses, in the period of about 5,000 years since the earliest domestication a great number of domestic horses of European origin have found their way to Central Asia and transformed the Asian stock. Moreover, side by side with these mixed stock horses were domesticated, have asserted as a counter-stock that closely resemble the Mongolian wild horse, not only in their skull form but in their colour as well. The

84

identity in colour is particularly striking in such colour variants as cannot be found among tarpans.

Among domestic horses of Kazakhstan and Bashkiria there are also individuals strikingly similar to the Przevalsky horse. They faithfully present the colour of the takhi, they have a well-developed dorsal stripe (individuals with a dorsal stripe are very highly valued by breeders practically throughout Central Asia), and they often have stripes on their legs. They only differ from the takhi in having long hanging manes and not short erect ones, and in that their tails are fully covered with long hair. At the end of the last century the Bashkirians were often given permission by the Governor of Orenburg to capture wild horses in the mountains of Kirghizia, and quite frequently returned with herds of them.

But why should the Mongolian wild horse not have been domesticated in Central Asia? Domestic mares could easily have been covered by wild stallions and borne their foals; or when a wild stallion died, his mares, left alone, might join some domestic herd. Even at the end of the last century and the beginning of ours it happened that Mongolian animal breeders would capture Przevalsky foals, admit them to their herds and rear them there: that is to say, they domesticated them. Besides—and this holds good in particular for prehistoric and early historic times, and for nomad herdsmen perhaps even later—animal keepers tried to increase the number of their domestic animals by any means, for livestock was the basis of "wealth" with them. We know of numerous instances of this from the prehistoric times of Europe, while isolated cases occurred in Roman times, and even in the Middle Ages: animal keepers tried to capture domesticable wild animals to increase their herds. Let us suppose that the earliest domestication of horses did not take place in the distribution area of Mongolian wild horses. However, when domestic horses had been introduced, say from Europe, the local people, seeing their usefulness, surely tried to domesticate local wild horses. The people had the necessary biological knowledge, since for hundreds and perhaps thousands of generations they had hunted wild horses and came to know them quite thoroughly. As has been shown by recent examples, Mongolian wild horses are domesticable. Why should they not be so? True, it does happen that of species quite close taxonomically one can be domesticated and the other one not (such as the case of the aurochs and the bison); but it has never happened that one subspecies of a species of animals could be domesticated and the other one not.

And, finally, we have one more cogent reason for supposing that the Mongolian wild horse has been domesticated. In the summer of 1963 a Mongolian-Hungarian archaeological expedition excavated a kurgan near Hana, on the right bank of the Hünij river in Mongolia. The kurgan was a burial ground of the Turkic period (seventh century A.D.) and it contained, among other things, the skeletons of two horses. Both skeletons were of adult stallions with withers heights of 135 and 136 cm. Not only in their size were the horses quite identical but in the proportions of their bodies as well. The two animals had obviously been the saddle horse and the led horse of the buried warrior, for in fighting with arrows it is very important that, when changing horses, the warrior should mount a horse of the same size and movement as the previous one. In size the two horses correspond with European animals of the Migration Period and of the early Middle Ages, and, at the same time, also with the average Mongolian horses of the Middle Ages. With respect to the structure of the skull, however, they differ

86

markedly from the former but correspond with recent Mongolian primitive horses. For want of adequate specimens it was not possible to compare the skulls with those of Mediaeval Mongolian horses; but they have been shown to tally with the skull of a horse born from a Przevalsky mare and sired by a Mongolian domestic stallion.

In summary, it can be stated that our supposition that Mongolian wild horses were domesticated is well founded. But whether the domestication took place in the territory of Mongolia and if so, when it was done for the first time, is impossible to say. However, this is only due to the inadequacy of archaeological excavations and the lack of animals' bones.

Towards the end of prehistoric times horse-keeping must have been fairly well developed in Mongolia, nor is it impossible that at the same period the beginnings of conscious and purposeful horse-breeding also appeared. This can be inferred from the horses' remains found at the Scythian (fifth century B.C.) kurgans of Pazyryk in the Altai.

These kurgans are above the snow-limit and therefore not only bones of horses were found—their number fluctuating between seven and fourteen per kurgan—but also mummified carcasses or, at least, parts of carcasses. This enabled V. O. Vitt, who studied the remains of horses, to draw some conclusions which other less fortunate zoologists had no possibility to infer.

In the kurgans two types (perhaps breeds) of horses were found: the common one with 130 cm withers height and the rarer one of 146–150 cm withers height. Of this latter type there was only one in each kurgan. In their well-fed condition and ornate trappings they must obviously have been the favourite saddle horses of the leader. Of the other horses, those buried in the early summer were very thin, the horizontal creases on their hooves testifying to long starvation in winter. Most of the horses were chestnut—in all shades of the colour; bay horses seldom occurred and there were no grey or piebald ones at all. No white stars could be discerned on the head, nor white stockings on the distal parts of the extremities.

Common Pazyryk horses had short and broad heads and in their form strongly resembled the Scythian horses represented on the vase of Tchertomlyk. The big horses had more elongated heads and nobler forms, though they were a far cry from the fine shape of present Arab horses. These horses had originated, in all probability, in Central Asia, though it cannot be ascertained from which territory. In Vitt's view they could by no means have been of Mongolian origin.

If these animals, excellent saddle horses under the conditions prevailing at that time—for according to finds in tombs they got through South-West Asia as far as Egypt—could not have originated from Mongolia, they could, no doubt, have exerted an effect on Mongolian horse-keeping.

On the other hand, the horses of the Huns, with which at least half of the world of that time was conquered, originated beyond dispute from Central Asia. Unfortunately hardly any bones of Hunnish horses have come down to us, but we know about them from Vegetius Renatus' description, according to which,

". . . for the purposes of war the Huns' horses are by far the most suitable, owing to their stamina, their working capacity and their endurance of cold and hunger. . . . The Huns' horses have big, crookedly curving heads and protruding eyes. Their nostrils are narrow, their jaws broad, their necks strong and rigid. Their manes fall down to their knees, their ribs are big, their spine curved, their tails bushy. They have very strong shinbones and small feet, the hooves being curved and broad. The soft parts are bulging and the whole body is angular. There is no fat on the rump, there are no bulges on the muscles, the body being long rather than tall. The trunk is rounded, the bones strong and the animals' thinness is striking. However, their beautiful characteristics, namely their calm nature, their cleverness and their ability to endure injuries very well, make one forget their ugly appearance."

This was written about the Huns' horses by a veterinary surgeon and a better opinion—concerning nature and performance, though not external appearance—cannot be given of a military horse. Incidentally, in ancient Chinese the name of wild horses and of the Huns' (Hiung-nu) horses was the same word, and this also makes one guess where the local origin of Hunnish horses must have been.

We have already heard of the horses of the Turkic period in Mongolia, but the opinion of the Mongolians' horses expressed by the Chinese Meng Hung in his book written in 1221 is very revealing: *

"The land of the Tartars is rich in water and grass suitable for sheep and horses. In the first year or two after birth their horses are ridden hard and trained in the grass-lands. Then they nourish them for three years and afterwards ride them again. Because they were trained early on they do not kick or bite. Herds are formed of thousands or hundreds, yet they are quiet with no neighing. When they dismount they do not need to tie up the horses. They will not stray. Their nature is extremely good. In the daytime they never feed them with

*After Wang Kuo-wei.

fodder. Only when night comes do they let them out to pasture. They pasture them on the steppe according to where the grass is green or withered. When morning comes they saddle and mount them. They never give them beans or grain at all. When they go on campaign every man has several horses, and they alternate horses daily, and for this reason the horses never get exhausted."

On the evidence of excavated extremity bones we also have an idea of what Mediaeval Mongolian horses were like.* In a thirteenth and fourteenth-century Mongolian settlement masses of bones of horses of 130–135 cm withers height were found; but among them was also a single bone of a horse of 160–165 cm withers height. This animal was big even by our present standards, and it was not a heavy "cold blood" horse!

The withers height of present Mongolian domestic horses is 120–130 cm. They are strong, thickset animals with short legs. They have relatively large heads with a short facial part and a broad forehead. However, individuals with long, ram-noses are not rare among them either. Their colour is very variable: generally bay, dun, chestnut or grey, but the proportion of piebald horses among them is strikingly high, perhaps connected with the ancient belief that piebald horses bring luck. Their accoutrement is very archaic and their saddles and bridles ornately studded with silver are still highly reminiscent of the Migration Period.

For the Mongolians the horse is, even today, first of all a means of transport: it is a saddle or a pack horse, and a draught animal of small carts. The people also eat its flesh, however, and fermented mare's milk is one of their favourite beverages.

*After Teichert, 1964.

The horse has a significant part in the Mongolians' religious cult as well as in their sagas. This is not surprising, as the horse meant more to the nomadic herdsman or warrior than any other of his domestic animals: it was his fellow-fighter, a faithful comrade and sometimes his only companion. This relationship was recognized in the fact that a warhorse was never killed but kept even when it became disabled or superannuated and was no longer of any practical use.

The dead warrior was very often buried together with his favourite steed; men of rank often with several of them. These horses were usually killed beside the tomb, their meat often being consumed at the funeral feast. The fell, with the skull and the feet left in it, was either stuck above the tomb stretched on poles or else laid inside—as described by Arab travellers or European missionaries and envoys who visited the Mongolian Empire in the Middle Ages. The custom of laying the horse's skull and feet in the tomb found its way with the peoples of the Migration Period to Europe, and spread westward as far as Denmark.

Shamans' horses had a special role, for they were thought to be endowed with singular magic powers. They appear in folktales, and strangely enough they too can be found in tombs of the Migration Period.

There is a long story attached to the buried shaman horses. Remains of lame horses have often been unearthed from Scythian tombs or tombs of the Migration Period, and attempts were made at explaining this somewhat strange phenomenon by suggesting that at the time of the burial the custom had already become obsolete and lost its content of belief. Only its form survived, so the relatives of the dead person tended to kill animals of little value to be buried with the deceased. The idea was also put forward that the lame horses may indeed have been the favourite horses of the warrior buried, which had been kept—out of reverence—long after they were too sick to work.

However a skeleton that points to quite a different explanation has been recently brought to light from an Avar tomb (eighth century A.D.). It is the skeleton of an adult stallion, which had the following pathological deformations: on the spinal column seventeen dorsal and lumbar vertebrae were grown together; the bones of the tarsus (hock) of the left hindleg were grown together in consequence of chronic deforming arthritis, so that the joint was almost completely rigid; and finally, in front of and beside the left external incisor there was a supernumerary incisor, quite clearly visible from the outside. Thus the animal was lame, and because its vertebrae had grown together it could move only with the greatest difficulty. The deformations of the vertebrae were so advanced that it must have taken several years for them to develop, and the animal could not have been used for any work at all for a long time. The presence of the extra incisor is especially intriguing because, according to Hungarian folklore, the shamans too had supernumerary teeth.

Shaman horses appear in Hungarian folk-tales too and they too have a supernumerary tooth. Further, in folk-tales the shaman horse (magic horse) is always in a poor condition, and in nearly every case lame—up to the point at which it turns into a magic horse, can revive its dead master with its bites, can speak, fly and perform miracles.

Thus for example, in the many tales about the guarding of the witch's three horses, the lad entering the service of the witch always chooses the poorest horse, which has disclosed to him the secret that it is a magic horse. In a variant, following the magic mare's advice, the lad asks only for a poor horse instead of wages; and in a third version the magic horse is definitely lame.

In one variant of the tale about the tree that reached the sky the lad asked the old woman to give him a horse so poor that it could hardly stand on its legs—and this animal too turned into a magic horse. In another version the little swineherd was tending three good foals and a fourth poor one, which could hardly totter and moreover had five legs. This one, too, was a magic horse.

The motif of magic horses appears generally in Hungarian folk-tales of eastern origin, in tales involving in some way Shamanist ideas. It can also be found in the tales of nearly all the peoples of Central Asia. The two essential characteristics of shaman horses correspond perfectly with the deformations observed on some of the lame horses found in tombs of eastern peoples of the Migration Period. Though not in so conspicuous a spot as on the horse of the Avar tomb mentioned above, a great many buried horses have supernumerary teeth. These are nothing but so-called wolf teeth, atavistic remains, sometimes in rudimentary form, of the first premolar of the original equids. Another characteristic quality of the magic horses of tales—a poor, lame condition—is also frequent among these horses buried together with their masters.

The diseased, lame horses were evidently the horses of shamans, animals to which weird magic powers were attributed and which were buried with their masters. There must have been some marks of identity on these horses—as there were on Apis bulls—to distinguish them as shaman horses. In all likelihood this was, first and foremost, their supernumerary tooth, but other external qualities may also have been prescribed. Nor is it impossible that their descent was the decisive point.

When concluding agreements the Mongolians usually sacrificed horses too. Thus, in *The Secret History of the Mongolians,* which is really a description of how Genghis Khan founded the Mongolian Empire, mention is made of how the slashing in two of a stallion and a mare solemnized the making of an oath. Centuries later the treaty between the Karakhin Mongolians and the Manchurians was sealed by the killing of a white horse and a black bull.

There is also another example of the extent to which the Mongolians' souls have been imbued with the love of the horse and the legends about it: one of the highest distinctions awarded by the Mongolian People's Republic is the Order of the Pole Star. According to Central Asian legends the pole star is really the end of a pole to which the hero ties his horse, or to which all dead horses are tethered in the other world.

# HOW MONGOLIAN WILD HORSES REACHED THE ZOOLOGICAL GARDENS OF EUROPE

When the scientific description of the Przevalsky horse had appeared and Colonel Przevalsky's travelogue, written in popular style, had been published, the new wild horse attracted the attention not only of the zoologists of Europe but also of animal-lovers. This meant—as we have learned before—first that more expeditions were organized to supply museums and collections with further skulls and fells; and then the idea arose to have live individuals of the new species captured and transferred to European zoos.

The Russian merchant N. I. Assanov was the first to conceive the idea in a realizable form. Assanov lived in the small town of Byjsk in the Province of Tomsk and, having for long had business connections with China, was pretty well versed in matters concerning Central Asia. In 1896 he mentioned his idea to the ethnographer D. A. Clemenz, who had stayed in Mongolia for five years. Clemenz had actually acquired a fell, attributed to a wild horse, but which in all likelihood was that of a hybrid animal, for the Zoological Museum of the Russian Academy of Sciences; as well as one for E. A. Büchner, leading zoologist of the Zoological Museum. But capturing wild horses meant operations on an altogether different scale. It meant the launching of a major expedition, and thus in turn demanded significant material investment. Thus they turned to F. E. Falz-Fein, a very rich landowner, with the result that on his estate at Askania Nova in the South of the Ukraine, an acclimatization park was founded which has since gained world renown.

Falz-Fein's own notes on the venture tell a somewhat different story, as can be read in the book his brother published in 1930:

"With the assistance of the zoologist Dr Büchner and the archaeologist Clemenz, who had many connections with the people of Mongolia, I started my endeavours as early as in 1896 to find persons there who could help me in acquiring wild horses. We sent presents to Mongolian princes and other different personages, and got into touch with Assanov, a merchant in Byjsk, Province Tomsk, who did business with China. It was with his help, though under great difficulties, that the first expeditions to the territories where the animals lived were equipped. Indeed, in 1897 we captured a number of young wild horses, but they all died because they had not been captured in the proper way. Thus I elaborated detailed prescriptions on this, and laid a special stress on the point that the animals were by no means to be caught by chasing them, but rather by shooting the mare, their mother. There were no milch-mares available from the Mongolians on the spot, so we had to purchase such mares in Byjsk as would give birth to their foals at the same time as the wild horses. The tame foals had to be killed in order that the tame mare might feed the captured foals; and to make the mare accept the wild foals we covered them with the fell of the tame ones. These rules not being adhered to the capture was again a failure; that is to say, all animals caught perished again. Now we instructed Assanov strictly to keep the prescriptions and, indeed, success ensued. The first foals were caught in the spring of 1899; six mares and a stallion. However, the stallion and one mare had to be left in Kobdo in Mongolia, because they were too weak to undertake the 500 km journey to Byjsk. The other five horses arrived at Novo-Alexeyevka, a station on the Kharkov-Sevastopol railway line, 70 km from Askania Nova, but there one of them died. At last, in the autumn, the other four young mares reached Askania Nova safe and sound. . . . The two animals left behind in Kobdo in 1899 were delivered to Assanov in Byjsk in the spring of 1900. There Ukhtomsky, a Russial official, saw them and persuaded Assanov to send them to the Tsar. Indeed, they were taken to Gatshina and were, by the Tsar's order, described by Academician Salensky. After some time the mare perished, but the stallion, a wonderful animal, was presented by the Tsar to me. As the capture of the animals had been initiated, further foals were captured for me in 1900, and they arrived in the autumn in Byjsk."

From the point of view of today's conservationist morality, this was no ideal method of catching individuals of a rare species on the point of extinction. It is understandable that zoological gardens and wealthy animal-lovers should have tried to acquire some of the newly discovered wild horses. It is also understandable that they endeavoured to capture foals, for they knew, on the basis of the Mongolians' experiences, that these would endure captivity more easily. It would even have been understandable if they had killed the leading stallion defending his group, for he would have been dangerous for the hunters, and a group of mares left without a stallion would anyhow be joined sooner or later by a lonely stallion. But to kill the mother mares with a view to catch the foals more easily was an appalling procedure indeed, since the number of wild horses was thus diminished not only by the captured foals. The killing of the mares put an end to the possibility of a number of further foals being born.

The capture of Przevalsky foals by the Falz-Fein expedition was described somewhat differently by D. A. Clemenz, the ethnographer who took part. And since he put his reminiscences to paper in 1903, and not after several years as Falz-Fein did in his recollections, the former seems to be more authentic. According to Clemenz the spring—the season for capturing wild horses—of 1897 was spent in preparations and in that year not a single wild foal was caught. Only in the next year did the actual work of capture begin. The expedition divided into two groups: one caught two Przevalsky horses in the Gobi of Djungharia and the other one four in the region where the river Emtkhe springs. However, for want of appropriate feeding—the members of the expedition tried to rear them on ewes' milk —these foals died while still in Mongolia. The skull and fell of three of them, along with those of an adult mare and a one-year-old stallion, reached the Zoological Museum of Saint Petersburg, but those of the other three must have been lost somewhere, because nothing has ben heard of them since.

According to Clemenz it was in 1899 that they succeeded in capturing more wild foals, of which only four survived. They spent the winter in Byjsk and got to Askania Nova only in 1900. (He makes no mention of the two foals presented to the Tsar.) Thus it seems to be probable that the

98

first living Przevalsky horses got to Europe in 1900 and not in 1899, the more so as another participant of the Falz-Fein expedition, the zoologist Büchner, indicated the same date in an article he too wrote in 1903.

In the monograph summarizing the history and research of the Przevalsky horse in the Soviet Union (the work of Garrutt, Sokolov and Salesskaya) too, 1900 is accepted as the date when the Mongolian wild horse was first introduced to Europe. This statement is based, in addition to the above sources, on the reminiscences of K. E. Siyenko, former custodian of the Askania Nova animals' park. The monograph seriously doubts whether the manner in which wild horses were captured was personally worked out by Falz-Fein, and points out Falz-Fein's lack of expert knowledge in suggesting (according to his book) that the domestic mares selected for feeding the wild foals should be wrapped in the fells of the killed wild mares. However this is probably a mistake of the translator's, for, as is evident from the text quoted at the beginning of this chapter, Falz-Fein suggested that the fell of the domestic mares' killed *foals* should be put on the wild *foals* they were to feed, to make the mares accept them instead of their own young. This is quite conceivable. Unfortunately, this part of the sentence in Falz-Fein's book is ambiguous.

Assanov presented two wild stallion foals to Moscow Zoo in 1901. One of them perhaps originated from the 1899 capture, whereas the other one was surely born in 1900 (side by side with the deal concluded with Falz-Fein, Assanov seems to have done private business on his own). A third filly foal born in 1901 got to Moscow Zoo in 1902. In all likelihood this one had also been captured by Assanov's hunters.

After the successful attempts in 1899 Assanov and his

99

group continued to capture Przevalsky foals. They seem to have acquired skill with practice, for the number of foals caught in 1900 (according to other sources in 1901) amounted to fifty-one, and of these twenty-eight (fifteen stallion foals and thirteen fillies) survived.

At that point Carl Hagenbeck, the most famous animal trader of all times, appeared on the scene. By the end of the century Hagenbeck's well-organized enterprise worked in as many as four continents supplying European and American zoos with exotic wild beasts—there are numerous species of wild animals that were first introduced to European zoological gardens by Hagenbeck.

With his excellent flair for business Hagenbeck immediately realized the possibilities that the introduction of Przevalsky foals to Europe offered, and endeavoured to organize their import. However differences soon arose between him and Falz-Fein who on the one hand did not want too many foals to reach the European market, since this would result in a fall in the value of those he kept in his own animal park; and on the other would have liked to keep in his own hands the European import of Mongolian wild horses. He had invested a great deal of money in expensive expeditions, so what he wanted was to reduce the prices at which he bought wild horses in Mongolia and at the same time to keep European sales prices at a high level. It is no surprise that he does not mention Hagenbeck, who soon snatched away this good business from him, in the kindest of terms:

"In the spring of 1901 I was in Antwerp, where I saw Hagenbeck. He would have liked to find out in what way I had acquired my wild horses. However, as he was by no means communicative in similar cases, I did not give him any information either. I attended an auction at the Zoological Garden and bought a number of animals. I also accepted Hagenbeck's offer to have one of his employees, who was about to travel to South Russia, bring the animals to Askania Nova. His employee interrogated my people about the circumstances under which the wild horses had been acquired in detail; then, in the autumn of 1901, he travelled direct to Byjsk and purchased from Assanov the twenty-eight animals meant for me, since, due to the illness of Dr Büchner, no instruction about their transport had arrived yet."

Now the question arises, how much of this is true and how much is due to the annoyance felt at the competitor's success. The snatching away of the twenty-eight Przevalsky foals by Hagenbeck's man was not fair indeed, though it was rather Assanov than Hagenbeck who was to blame. However, the fact that Assanov dared to sell to Hagenbeck the foals meant for Falz-Fein points to the fact that he was not operating simply with Falz-Fein's money as his principal agent, but was an independent entrepreneur. In this case he, as a businessman, simply sold his goods to the buyer who paid more. Finally, the possibility cannot be left out of consideration that Falz-Fein, relying too heavily on his monopoly position, kept Assanov waiting for his offer too long in order to cut his prices; and that all of a sudden the competitor Hagenbeck appeared and bought the foals.

The other part of the story, concerning the information on the acquisition of Przevalsky horses fraudulently obtained, does not sound untrue. What is the strangest in the whole matter is that this strategy should have been necessary, since Assanov had offered for sale the foals he had captured to various European zoological gardens, and so Hagenbeck too could have learned about the source. In some way or other, this must have escaped his attention. In his reminiscences Hagenbeck himself gave the same version of how he had found out the secret source where Przevalsky foals could be obtained:

"First of all Grieger (one of Hagenbeck's cleverest agents) escorted a consignment of animals to Mr Falz-Fein to South Russia. This lover of animals, with reason jealous of his treasures, did not divulge the information desired. Only by roundabout means did my agent find out that the places where wild horses could be caught were in the vicinity of Kobdo, below the northern slopes of the Altai Mountains. With the geographical fingerpost gained Grieger happily travelled to Petersburg to prepare there the 4,000 km journey into Central Mongolia. . . ."

Long pages follow describing the adventures of Hagenbeck's two agents. They encounter all kinds of experiences: a journey on the Trans-Siberian railway, a trip by sledge from the Ob to Byjsk, the frontier town of Russia; 900 km covered on camel back to Kobdo, a short description of the town of Kobdo; an introduction to the customs of the local Mongolians; the organization of the hunting caravan, the hunt and the capture of wild horses and, finally, a description of their transport home. The only defect of the romantic story is that all that was described after the writer's stay at the town of Byjsk was fiction. It is possible that the agents appropriated the actual adventures of other Central Asian expeditions of the firm Hagenbeck, and that the events had really taken place. But they did not take place on this journey, for one thing is certain: they themselves got only as far as Byjsk in connexion with the business of wild horses, and it was there that they bought all the twenty-eight

Przevalsky foals from Assanov. Clemenz was already aware of this in 1903 and obviously it was from him, one of the leading members of the Falz-Fein–Assanov–Clemenz–Büchner venture, that Falz-Fein got his information. Whether this information never reached Hagenbeck, or, if it did, why he persisted in his romantic biography in using the tale his men had told him, we cannot guess today.

Nevertheless, one essential inference must be drawn from the above story: namely that the descriptions Hagenbeck's men gave of the habitat, the customs and way of life of Mongolian wild horses were not based on their own observations. They must have heard everything from Assanov, on the basis of information given by local Mongolian hunters. So use of these pieces of information needs particular caution.

In any case, the speed with which these men carried out the import of the first wild horses demonstrates the extraordinary expertness and efficiency of Hagenbeck's organization. In the spring of 1901 Hagenbeck met Falz-Fein; soon afterwards his men found out where Przevalsky foals could be acquired, travelled to the spot, bought twenty-eight foals from Assanov and arrived with them in Hamburg in October of the same year, bringing along all the twenty-eight foals alive.

In the autumn of 1902 Hagenbeck's men imported a further eleven wild horse foals, probably again purchased from Assanov. Their proportion with respect to sex is not exactly known, but the whole import was not a great success as several animals perished soon after their arrival. Possibly this was due to the fact that the foals of the first consignment, having spent a longer time with Assanov, who was bargaining for quite a long time with Falz-Fein, had got better acclimatized and thus could bear the stress of travelling, whereas the animals of the second lot were transported to Hamburg right away. The death of a considerable number of foals is suggested by the fact that at that same time the fell or skull of several Przevalsky horses born in free nature found their way to different German museums. Erna Mohr supposed that along with the living foals Hagenbeck's men had brought with them the fell and skulls of further young animals as well as of adult ones, because in collections of natural history all the world over there are more fells and skulls of wild horses born in Mongolia to be seen than the number of imported animals. This assumption is confirmed by the fact that the name of Umlauff, dealer in natural history specimens and connected with Hagenbeck, is often to be found in inventories of museums among the sellers of objects purchased.

But Falz-Fein seems not to have given up the import of Przevalsky foals either, although his transactions were not of the magnitude of Hagenbeck's. He had a group of two mares and a stallion brought to Askania Nova in 1902 and another one comprising two mares and a hybrid stallion early in 1904. These were again animals captured by Assanov's men. But after this Assanov discontinued the capture of wild horses, which had evidently become so rare that to capture further foals would have involved very high costs.

Only after the second world war did a further Mongolian wild horse caught in free nature find its way to Europe. The mare Orlitza III-Mongol captured in the Baytag-Bogdo mountains in 1947 was transported to Askania Nova in 1957. Today it is the only living Mongolian wild horse caught in its original habitat in a European animal park.

To summarize, F. Falz-Fein was the first man to import Mongolian wild horses; but C. Hagenbeck's contribution in transferring this extraordinarily interesting rarity of nature to our zoological gardens is also outstanding. In addition to their work that of N. I. Assanov is important too, for he did the work of actual organization on the spot; and it was through his mediation that all the early consignments of imported foals were realized.

The Przevalsky foals transported to Europe found owners very quickly. This is not surprising since the discovery of the Mongolian wild horse created a sensation among European nature lovers. It is characteristic that it was on the commission of the second Duke of Bedford that Hagenbeck sent his men to Central Asia, so the risks he took personally were not too great; he must have been sure that the imported wild foals could be sold.

And indeed the foals were sold. Out of the first consignment the Duke of Bedford bought five stallions and seven mares for his animal park at Woburn. Another pair found its way to London Zoo and was joined later by a further pair, the present of W. Rothschild. A breeder named Blaauw purchased another pair from the Dutch Goilust, and further pairs found their way to the zoological gardens of Halle, Berlin and New York (Bronx). The last seem not to have fared well in New York, because they were soon transferred to Cincinnati. One stallion was bought by the Paris Zoo. We do not know anything about the remaining three stallions.

With the second consignment Hagenbeck was not so lucky. Five of the eleven foals (three stallions and two mares) died not long after their arrival in Hamburg. A pair of the surviving ones was purchased by each of the Bronx and Edinburgh Zoos; one stallion got to Amsterdam Zoo and a mare remained with Hagenbeck.

However, the Mongolian wild foals that had been transferred to Europe were not meant only for display in zoological gardens. Breeding was also attempted and these attempts were successful. Growing up, most of the foals were able to produce progeny and young were soon born. Four centres of breeding Przevalsky horses emerged in Europe: in Askania Nova, in Woburn, in Berlin–Hellabrunn and in Prague, and a fifth came into being at Catskill in America after the second world war. Of course in other zoological gardens and animal parks too Przevalsky horses were bred, and they found their way to all continents except Africa—but always in small numbers only. On the other hand, the four centres mentioned above have had a decisive significance in the European breeding of Mongolian wild horses, increasing the number of wild horses descended from imported ones, supplying them to many other zoos and effectively ensuring the survival of Mongolian wild horses.

## THE WILD HORSES IN CAPTIVITY

A great many Russian and Soviet authors have written about the breeding of wild horses in Askania Nova, while the history of the three other centres and the history of Mongolian wild horses in European zoological gardens in general has been elaborated by Erna Mohr. This was practically her whole life's work, and the fact that she was personally acquainted not only with the heads of the institutions in question but with nearly all wild horses in Europe, made her history as complete a work as possible. The stud-book of Przevalsky horses was also a highly useful initiative of hers; and since her death Prague Zoo has continued to register entries in the stud-book. The history of the four breeding centres outlined here is mostly based on her works.

Askania Nova is in the Tchapli sector of Kherson province of the South Ukraine, that is to say not in the Crimea, as has been erroneously claimed by several authors, who based their statement on the fact that the territory used to belong to the Province of Tauria, which also included regions north of the Crimea. The Falz-Fein family was of German origin (their name was Pfalz-Fein before it was changed into the Russian form). The Falz-Feins bought the big estate in 1856 from the Princes of Anhalt-Köthe, and a later offspring of the family, Friedrich (or, as he is often called in Russian and

Soviet literature, Fyodor Eduardovitch) Falz-Fein, decided in the second half of the last century to establish an animal park there, first of all for species that would feel the place their habitat. Later the animal park grew into a famous research institute for acclimatization and animal breeding.

In the beginning the keeping of Mongolian wild horses in Askania Nova did not look very successful. Of the first consignment comprising four mares born in 1899 and arriving there in the first months of 1900 (or at the end of 1899), only one, Staraya I, grew up and lived sixteen years. One died soon after its arrival, another one in the same year and the third at an unknown date. Of the second consignment of three animals which arrived in 1902, one mare soon died, the stallion passed away in the fifth year of his age and only the second mare, Staraya I, lived till 1915. And finally, one of the mares of the third, 1904, consignment died soon after its arrival and the other at the age of six; the hybrid stallion imported together with them died at the age of five years without being used for breeding.

Thus breeding could only be started when the surviving Przevalsky horse of the two presented to the Tsar, the stallion Waska, got to Askania Nova at the age of five years in May 1904. This stallion was an extraordinarily characteristic individual of Mongolian wild horses; though in the beginning he was irascible and vehement, he became so tame that later he could be used for riding. A picture of this long-headed, short-trunked stallion with a horseman in a fur-hat on his back is to be seen in practically every book on wild horses, as a typical representative of the Przevalsky horse. Up to his death in 1915 Waska was used for breeding purposes with two mares.

By 1918 the number of pure-blood Przevalsky horses in Askania Nova had risen to six, and these horses—thanks to the self-sacrificing work of the park's personnel and indeed to the extraordinary stamina of Przevalsky horses—not only survived the turbulent times of the civil war following the October revolution, but their number actually rose, and by September 1921 there were as many as eight pure-blood Przevalsky horses in the park. Breeding continued to be very successful and between 1905 and 1940 there were as many as thirty-seven pure-blood Przevalsky foals born in Askania Nova, without the introduction of any further horses for breeding purposes. Among the Przevalsky horses born in Askania Nova up to the 1st of January 1970 four died one day after their birth, eight before reaching the age of one year, six between the ages of one and three years, six between three and ten years of age, two between twenty and twenty-five years of age, and five of them are still alive. Eleven pure-blooded Przevalsky horses have been sold to various zoological gardens of Europe. (Though as far as the pure blood of some of them is concerned strong doubts have recently arisen).

In Askania Nova not only pure-blood Mongolian horses were bred; they were also cross-bred with domestic horses and with zebras. In both cases cross-breeding proved to be successful.

The second world war put an end to the whole stud of Askania Nova, of which only a mare of one-eighth blood and the zebroids survived. In 1948 Robert, a five-year-old pure-blood Przevalsky stallion, was brought there from Hellabrunn. Under the name of Orlik-Robert he first covered domestic mares, then, since 1957, he sired several offspring covering the mare Orlitza III-Mongol, an animal imported from Mongolia. In recent years a purposeful exchange has been pursued between Askania Nova, Prague and Hellabrunn, in order to introduce new blood into Przevalsky horses.

We know far less about the famous Woburn stud. The reason for this is that when in 1955 the last stallion died there, all the breeding records were also destroyed. So it is only indirectly that one can draw inferences on breeding there, relying on the data of the animals that found their way from Woburn to various zoological gardens of Europe and America.

Between 1919 and 1942 it is known that three mares and three stallions reached London Zoo from Woburn, some as presents and some on loan. It was also from Woburn that a mare got to the Paris Zoo in 1906, to be a mate of the stallion originating from the first Hagenbeck consignment. In 1911 the zoological garden of Adelaide purchased a stallion from Woburn, and in 1922 the animal park of Goilust. Erna Mohr assumed that these animals constituted but a small part of the progeny born at Woburn, which seems to be quite reasonable, for that animal park had the greatest stock to start breeding with.

The centres of Mongolian wild horse breeding in Berlin and Hellabrunn became one unit, for the simple reason that the directors of each were both members of the famous Heck dynasty, and the two zoos often exchanged animals or loaned them to each other. It was in the Berlin Zoo that the breeding of Przevalsky horses was begun, though not with the pair that was acquired in 1901 from the first consignment of Hagenbeck's. These animals died without any progeny, though both were long-lived: the mare died at the age of fifteen years and the stallion at twenty-five. But in 1926 the Zoo acquired from Askania Nova the six-year-old stallion Pascha (there Minoi), and in 1927 the mare Bella (there Orlitza II), which was one year old. They proved to be excellent animals for breeding and produced as many as six foals. With the exception of one, which was one day old when it died, these foals proved to be outstandingly fit for life. Only one stallion died a natural death at the age of two years; one of the mares was fourteen, a stallion six and another mare three years of age when they fell victim at Schorfheide to the events at the end of the second world war. With them the Berlin herd came to an end.

The founding stallion of the Berlin branch, Pascha, and his first filly foal, Lori, which was born in 1931, were sent for a time to Hellabrunn, near Munich, and that is how the Hellabrunn branch came into being. Two mares of Prague Zoo were also transferred there and so, in 1938, was a stallion of one year and a half, born at Whipsnade Zoo. Covered by Pascha, Lori and her daughter Ella, who represented the Askania Nova line together with the two mares of Prague (Bessie and Selma) each gave birth to five foals. Then Lori and Pascha returned to Berlin and from there to Schorfheide, where they perished together with the rest of the Berlin Przevalsky horses in 1945. The Hellabrunn branch continued to develop undisturbed and numerous animals of its progeny found their way to zoos both in Europe and in America. Thus it was with a Hellabrunn stallion that the breeding of Mongolian wild horses was resumed in Askania Nova, but wild horses got to Rome, Chicago and Copenhagen too, and a smaller herd was started on the famous Catskill Game Farm as well.

It is characteristic of the stamina of the Hellabrunn branch that—according to the data of the stud-book of Przevalsky horses—among the Mongolian wild horses born there between June 14th 1935 and May 25th 1969 only seven died when they were one day old and five before reaching the age of one year. Eight lived for four to ten years, six for eleven to twenty and one for twenty-three years. Among the Przevalsky horses born at Hellabrunn and still alive, there is one twenty-five years old, two of twenty-four, one each of twenty-two, twenty and nineteen years, two each of eighteen and sixteen years, one each of fourteen, thirteen and twelve years, two of ten years, one each of nine, eight, seven and six years, two of five years, one of four years, two each of three and two years and one of one year.

The Berlin branch has never been revived, though the zoos both of East and West Berlin have Mongolian wild horses today.

The breeding of Przevalsky horses in Prague also has time-honoured traditions to look back upon. Its origin can be traced back to Halle, for the famous zoological garden of Halle University also acquired a pair of foals of the first Hagenbeck consignment. They were made to breed not only between each other; the stallion was also used for cross-breeding with domestic mares. But this stallion died in 1908 without having sired a pure-blood stallion. So his son born from a chestnut Mongolian domestic mare was used for breeding purposes. This meant that domestic blood got into the Halle branch as well as into the Prague one since it originated from the former.

At that time and since, this policy aroused strong emotions among zoologists and breeders. Some authorities even question whether members of the Halle-Prague branch in whose family tree the Halle 1 stallion, an offspring of the Mongolian domestic mare, appears can be considered Przevalsky horses at all. Some of them censured Erna Mohr, who had initiated the stud-book of Przevalsky horses, for having passed over this fact by simply registering it and entering the animals in question into the stud-book. These authors compared the question with that of the European bisons whom Erna Mohr had refused to enter into her stud-book of bisons because the blood of these animals contained that of American bisons or

112

of steppe cattle. And since, through the individuals originating from the Prague stud, a minimal percentage of domestic blood has found its way to a great many European wild horses (thus, first of all into one of the Munich lines), they suggested that these animals be treated in the stud-book as a strictly separate line, segregated from pure-blooded Przevalsky horses; and that the two lines should by no means be mixed.

To judge the question in this manner appears to be a bit too severe. As we have seen above, in free nature too domestic blood could very easily get into Mongolian wild horses. Therefore nobody can guarantee that a Przevalsky foal captured in free nature does not contain a single drop of domestic blood. What can we do in such a case? At most we can decide whether, on grounds of the phenotype, the exterior of the animal, we accept it as a wild horse or not. And he who has ever dealt with wild horses or primitive domestic ones can tell how difficult this is in some cases. Foals suspected of having some domestic blood incidentally occurred among those imported by Hagenbeck too.

Similarly too strict is the comparison of the problem with the case of the European bison. According to the concepts of modern biology a given domestic species and the wild animal of which it was domesticated constitute a single species. Ever since the beginning of domestication domestic animals and their wild forms have cross-bred and this has been the case with the wild horse and the domestic one ever since prehistoric times. The European bison's case, on the other hand, is quite different, for there the cross-breeding did not take place with domesticated individuals of the same species, but, in the case of the American bison, with another species: steppe cattle, though this other species definitely belongs to another subgenus too. This is the same case as a wild horse being cross-bred with a zebra or an ass: by no means could such offspring be entered into the stud-book of Przevalsky horses.

On the other hand, those who have raised the question are right in endeavouring to ensure that, even if cross-breeding has taken place, no domestic blood should be introduced into the few surviving wild horses intentionally. Chromosome investigations are for the time being at an initial stage and the genetic background has not been clarified yet. It would be a pity to disturb the picture that is now slowly taking shape.

In Prague the breeding of Mongolian wild horses began with the four-year-old stallion Ali bought in Halle in 1921, and with two mares also bought there in 1923: four-year-old Minka and two-year-old Halle 9. Soon after her arrival in Prague this latter died. The surviving pair was taken over by the Zootechnical Institute of the Agricultural Academy of Prague and transferred to its model farm for educational purposes. There, in the country, they produced four foals within four years. The first of them died at birth, the remaining three were sold to Hellabrunn. One broke the nape of her neck on the way and died, but the other two—Bessie and Selma already mentioned—arrived safe and sound and became the mares founding the Prague line of the Hellabrunn stud.

In 1932 Ali and Minka got to Prague Zoo and had a filly foal; then, in 1933, the stallion died. In 1934 the stallion Horymir was transferred from Washington to Prague and he—an animal of excellent shape—sired numerous foals until his death in 1944. After his death it was only in 1950 that Prague Zoo acquired a new stallion—Uran—able to produce progeny. From that time on there have been foals born there practically every year. In general this good breeding capacity is characteristic of the Prague herd. A good example of this is Minka, who gave birth to a foal at the age of twenty-four years, while Vlasta and Helus were each twenty-three when their last foals were born. The two former mares had six foals each, whereas Vlasta and Lucka had thirteen foals each according to the Przevalsky horse stud-book.

Of the Mongolian wild horses born to the Prague herd between 1928 and June 14th 1969, six died between one and three days of age and one before reaching its first year. Fourteen lived one to three years, nine four to ten years, four eleven to twenty and four twenty-one to twenty-nine years. Among the Przevalsky horses born in Prague and alive on January 1st 1970 there was one of twenty-six years, two of twenty, one of eighteen, one of seventeen, two of sixteen, two of fourteen, one of twelve, four of eleven, four of ten, three of nine, three of eight, six of seven, six of six, four of five, four of four, four of three years of age, as well as three of two years and three of one year.

Among all zoological gardens of the world at present, the Prague Zoo possesses the greatest number of Przevalsky horses, and to the present total must still be added the Mongolian wild horses born there but which have found their way to numerous zoos of the world.

Catskill Game Farm, in up-state New York, has a shorter past to look back upon than any of the above-mentioned four breeding centres. However, it was with such intensity that breeding was started there, and it has been so successful since, that by now the studfarm has become one of the most significant and has—side by side with Prague Zoo—the greatest number of wild horses.

Breeding began at Catskill only in 1956 when Roland Linde-mann bought six mares and four stallions from Hellabrunn, all of the animals belonging to the Askania line. That is to say they were pure-blood Przevalsky horses without any Prague blood in them and thus they could meet the very highest breeding requirements. One of the stallions perished during transport but the others arrived safe and sound in November, and in the August of the following year Berta gave birth to a healthy filly foal (Rolinda = 227 Catskill), proving that she had been in foal during the trip.

In 1957 a further pair, and in 1963 a stallion and two mares, were taken over from Hellabrunn by Catskill, though the stallion was soon given to Los Angeles. These animals too belonged to the Askania line.

Between August 20th 1957 and May 21st 1969 forty-three foals were born by the animals imported to Catskill. It is characteristic of the good breeding results that in 1961 and 1967 the Catskill mares gave birth to six foals and in 1966 to seven. Seven of the foals died between the ages of one and ten days, one was six months old, one two years, and five between the ages of four and ten years; but the others are still alive. The animals brought from Hellabrunn proved to be very long-lived too. Though one of them died at the age of one year and a half, two others lived seven and eight years respectively, the third eleven years and a fourth eighteen. Among those alive on January 1st 1970, the stallion Sigi is twenty and Severin twenty-four years of age, while the mare Belle is eighteen and Berta twenty-five years old.

At present Mongolian wild horses are to be found in forty-three zoos of Europe and America. It is interesting that in Mongolia, the original home of the Przevalsky horse, we do not know for certain of the existence of a single living wild horse in captivity. In his letter on his trip to Mongolia Dr C. Purkyne, Director of Prague Zoo, mentioned to Erna Mohr a Przevalsky horse he had seen in Ulan Bator. This datum seems not to have been confirmed as that animal is not indicated in the stud-book of Przevalsky horses. Possibly it was not a pure-blood Przevalsky horse but only a bastard, for such were rather frequently found in Mongolia. At the 1959 Prague symposium dealing with the Przevalsky horse the Director of Yerevan Zoo mentioned in his contribution that the Zoo had had a Przevalsky stallion (Tornado= Vasik, an animal of Prague origin), which, however, got to Askania Nova in 1960 and to Moscow in 1964, where it is still alive. In several Australian zoological gardens (Adelaide, Sydney, Perth) there used to be lonely Przevalsky horses or pairs for breeding, which in Sydney indeed produced progeny. But in 1958 the last wild stallion died there and since then no further wild horses have been introduced to Australia. And so far no Mongolian wild horses have been introduced to African zoos.

According to the stud-book of Przevalsky horses there were on January 1st 1970, 161 Mongolian wild horses (sixty-seven stallions and ninety-four mares) in different zoos and animal parks. A distribution chart appears on pages 118 and 119.

Finally we should like to correct three errors in the 1970 edition of the stud-book of Przevalsky horses: first, according to the introductory table, but not according to the stud-book, there lives at Catskill the mare Rolanda 168. The same discrepancy applies—the other way round—to the mare Durose 170. We assume that the data of the stud-book are correct and the introductory table contains printers' errors. Second, with respect to the stallion Hamlet 325, which came to Budapest from Prague, the data in the introductory table are correct, which becomes evident if we consider item 9 of the stud-book, according to which the stallion which died in 1954 got to Budapest Zoo in 1966. When this manuscript was completed on June 28th 1970 the stallion was still alive.

| Place | Number of animals | Stallion | Year of birth | Mare | Year of birth |
|---|---|---|---|---|---|
| Aalborg | 2 | 1 | 1960 | 1 | 1966 |
| Amsterdam | 2 | 1 | 1958 | 1 | 1966 |
| Antwerp | 5 | 2 | 1954, 1960 | 3 | 1954, 1958, 1963 |
| Arnhem | 2 | 1 | 1964 | 1 | 1966 |
| Askania Nova | 7 | 4 | 1961, 1963, 1964, 1968 | 3 | 1947, 1960, 1963 |
| Barcelona | 3 | 1 | 1964 | 2 | 1958, 1964 |
| Barnesville | 1 | 0 | | 1 | 1963 |
| Berlin–East | 3 | 1 | 1961 | 2 | 1956, 1967 |
| Berlin–West | 2 | 1 | 1960 | 1 | 1959 |
| Bojnice | 3 | 1 | 1962 | 2 | 1960, 1968 |
| Brno | 3 | 2 | 1961, 1968 | 1 | 1963 |
| Budapest | 1 | 1 | 1964 | 0 | |
| Catskill | 16 | 5 | 1946, 1956, 1965, 1966, 1968 | 11 | 1945, 1952, 1956, 1958, 1960, 1961, 1961, 1962, 1962, 1962, 1969 |
| Chicago | 3 | 2 | 1951, 1967 | 1 | 1967 |
| Cologne | 4 | 1 | 1963 | 3 | 1963, 1968, 1969 |
| Colwyn Bay | 1 | 1 | 1966 | 0 | |
| Copenhagen | 5 | 1 | 1954 | 4 | 1954, 1962, 1963, 1966 |
| Eberswalde | 1 | 1 | 1963 | 0 | |
| Edmonton | 2 | 1 | 1963 | 1 | 1963 |
| Falkesstein | 1 | 1 | 1966 | 0 | |
| Havana | 2 | 1 | 1967 | 1 | 1963 |
| Karlsruhe | 3 | 2 | 1959, 1963 | 1 | 1962 |

| Place | Number of animals | Stallion | Year of birth | Mare | Year of birth |
|---|---|---|---|---|---|
| Langenfeld | 1 | 1 | 1967 | 0 | |
| Leipzig | 3 | 1 | 1967 | 2 | 1961, 1966 |
| Lexington | 1 | 1 | 1963 | 0 | |
| London (Aspinall) | 2 | 1 | 1969 | 1 | 1969 |
| London (Zoo) | 3 | 2 | 1957, 1968 | 1 | 1960 |
| Los Angeles | 2 | 1 | 1960 | 1 | 1961 |
| Moscow | 1 | 1 | 1950 | 0 | |
| Munich | 10 | 4 | 1948, 1963, 1968, 1969 | 6 | 1946, 1952, 1957, 1965, 1965, 1967 |
| New York | 3 | 1 | 1967 | 2 | 1967, 1967 |
| Nuremberg | 4 | 1 | 1965 | 3 | 1964, 1965, 1967 |
| Owslebury | 4 | 1 | 1968 | 3 | 1968, 1968, 1969 |
| Paris | 5 | 2 | 1959, 1962 | 3 | 1957, 1966, 1967 |
| Prague | 16 | 4 | 1944, 1962, 1963, 1964 | 12 | 1950, 1954, 1956, 1958, 1959, 1959, 1959, 1960, 1962, 1965, 1967, 1969 |
| Rotterdam | 9 | 3 | 1953, 1960, 1968 | 6 | 1956, 1960, 1964, 1964, 1967, 1969 |
| Salzburg | 2 | 1 | 1967 | 1 | 1968 |
| San Diego | 4 | 1 | 1964 | 3 | 1964, 1965, 1969 |
| Tallinn | 2 | 1 | 1965 | 1 | 1966 |
| Warsaw | 3 | 2 | 1962, 1969 | 1 | 1964 |
| Washington | 1 | 1 | 1950 | 0 | |
| Wassenaar | 3 | 1 | 1961 | 2 | 1963, 1967 |
| Whipsnade | 10 | 4 | 1960, 1968, 1969 | 6 | 1952, 1961, 1963, 1966, 1968, 1969 |

Third, the Catskill horse Roland 320 is, in all likelihood, not a mare as indicated in the stud-book but a stallion. Apart from its name this becomes evident from the introductory table, which would otherwise not be correct since it indicates one stallion and three mares to be living at San Diego Zoo at present.

# THE FUTURE OF THE MONGOLIAN WILD HORSE

We can now conclude that two processes are taking place in the stock of Przevalsky horses of the world: the number of animals living in free nature is decreasing, while that of wild horses in captivity, in zoological gardens and animal parks, is growing steadily.

Proof of the diminishing in numbers of Mongolian wild horses in free nature is the circumstance that in its distribution area not a single individual had been seen by researchers for so many years that it was a veritable sensation when Z. Kaszab encountered a group in 1966. But it is now absolutely certain that wild horses are not extinct in free nature.

So far no well organized venture to find wild horses in South-West Mongolia near the Chinese frontier and beyond the frontier in Djungharia has been launched. Considering the vast extent of the area to be explored, as well as the inconceivable difficulties of the terrain, an expedition of a couple of overland cars cannot be expected to achieve major results. But keeping a bigger expedition moving would also be hard if we consider only the problems of fuel supply. The only expedient solution would be to explore the territory by air. For this purpose helicopters or small aircraft of low speed, airplanes that need short runways, would be most suitable. On the other hand, to set up such an expedition would be a very costly business, which would seem only to be feasible by international co-operation, probably within the framework of UNESCO.

The following figures give a good idea of the quick proliferation of Przevalsky horses in zoos: at the end of 1958 there lived fifty-six Mongolian wild horses in captivity. By the beginning of 1965, the time of the second symposium on Przevalsky horses, their number had risen nearly twofold: to 110. And by the end of 1969 there were altogether 161 Mongolian wild horses living in zoological gardens.

This increase in the number of Przevalsky horses in zoos can be traced back to two causes. One is that breeders are now thoroughly familiar with the biology and physiology of wild horses. On the basis of this knowledge they have succeeded in ensuring for the wild horses in captivity conditions of life approaching the ideal. In such circumstances breeding results have markedly improved, and mares giving birth to a foal almost annually, and rearing them successfully, are no longer rare.

The other reason is that in zoological gardens protection of wild horses' health has now reached a very high level. Examining the death statistics of Przevalsky horses' breeding centres we can easily deduce that in the Mongolian wild horse's life the few days right after birth are the most critical, for it is then that the greatest number of foals perish. This is due, first and foremost, to lack of vitamins, for only a very small quantity of vitamins get into the foetus from the mother's body through the placenta. On account of the lack of vitamins a great many specific germs, threatening foals' lives, such as streptococci, coli-bacilli and other microorganisms may easily overcome the resistance of the young organism. Zoos try to prevent the avitaminosis and the infections of the first days by administering various vitamin preparations and combined sera. The good results achieved by this are proved by the attainments of Berlin Zoo where, thanks to the above treatment, not a single foal among the equids (Przevalsky horses, onagers, zebras) died between 1960 and 1964.

Along with appropriate circumstances of keeping and foddering, veterinary service plays a large part in enabling wild horses to live to advanced ages in zoos, as well as in guarding their health so that they are able to produce progeny for a long time. Among Mongolian wild horses kept in captivity, stallions progenitive, and mares able to conceive after the twentieth year of their age are no longer rare.

This again gives rise to the question whether, setting out from the present stock of Przevalsky horses, the survival of the Mongolian wild horse can now be assured. The answer can only be in the affirmative, particularly if we consider that the enterprise to save the European bison was started with fifty-four progenitive individuals in 1922 and, in spite of the fact that the second world war inflicted serious injuries on the stock, their number had risen to 255 in Poland alone by the end of 1966.

The situation is much better with respect to the Mongolian wild horse. Here—notwithstanding the fact that, for the time being, we can rely only on wild horses living in captivity—the stock from which to start is much bigger. And there is another essential advantage: the descent of the stock of wild horses is very well known and the degree of kinship can be exactly stated with every animal. Thus breeding between related animals and the danger of degeneration can easily be avoided.

On the other hand, the menace of domestication can easily arise in the case of Mongolian wild horses. Domestication is a very peculiar process. Generally, it is commenced by man, who utilizes for his own advantage the individuals of certain species of animals. But whether a species of wild animals can be domesticated or not does not depend only on man. Obviously there is some psychological difference between domesticable and non-domesticable species of wild animals. There is a certain psychological quality in the domesticable species—or else a lack of it—which renders domestication possible. It is also certain that this quality is not connected with the systematic position of the species in question; for on the one hand domesticable animals belong to the most varied taxonomical groups, and on the other it often happens that of two species very close to each other in taxonomy, one can be domesticated whilst the other cannot. Suffice it to mention in this connection that among the four subgenera of recent equids only horses and asses are domesticable, but half-asses and zebras are not; or that the bezoar-goat is domesticable but its close relative the ibex is not.

The bison is a non-domesticable species (though taxonomically and osteologically it is quite close to cattle!), but the wild horse is. Thus the danger of domestication has not arisen with bisons kept in captivity, but it may easily loom with Mongolian wild horses in zoos. When kept in zoos domesticable wild animals may soon show transformations of the kind caused by domestication. Such tendencies are to be found for example among wolves kept in captivity. It is not impossible that the Przevalsky horses in zoological gardens mentioned by Mohr, which have light manes, stars on their foreheads, and light or dark spots in the coats, were presenting phenomena of domestication.

No doubt animals kept in captivity are of decisive significance to the survival of the Mongolian wild horse, for their breeding can be carried out purposefully under human control; but the stock living in free nature must not be forgotten either. It is unquestionable that if appropriate protective measures are applied their number can be maintained or even increased.

To ensure watering-places is a basic condition for ensuring the survival of Mongolian wild horses in free nature. It is a well-known fact that the numbers of wild horses have fallen to a catastrophic extent in South-West Mongolia since nomadic animal-keepers invaded with their livestock territories that had not been used by herders before—that is to say regions that had been the last sanctuaries of Przevalsky horses. These nomads occupied the natural springs and wells to be found there and ousted the wild horses, which are exceedingly timid. Thus if we want to preserve wild horses in free nature we must maintain for them certain places where they can find water.

It goes without saying that this is an extraordinarily difficult problem, for the interests of nature conservation clash with those of nomadic animal-keepers. We do not know, however, whether Bannikov's suggestion, according to which a wildlife refuge should be demarcated in the Takhiyn Shara nuru or the Baytag-Bogdo chain of mountains, where wild horses could live undisturbed, would be successful. Perhaps it would be even more expedient if, in forming such a wildlife refuge, some wells were drilled as well. In recent years large-scale prospecting has been pursued in Mongolia to find water reserves concealed underground. At present this is first of all profitable for livestock-keeping and to a lesser extent for agriculture. It is highly probable that by the drilling only of a few wells (and ensuring their operation) a far greater number of protected animals would live in the future wildlife refuge area than before. And it is quite certain that the still-existing groups of wild horses would, after a time, discover the territory where they could live undisturbed by man, and withdraw there. Thus it would also become easier to control them and to keep them in evidence.

However strange this may sound, the greatest obstacle to establishing a wildlife refuge is the fact that the area is so sparsely populated. Under conditions prevailing in Mongolia it is simply impossible to surround with a fence such a vast reserve and to keep the fence in good repair. It would also be difficult to provide for an adequate number of guards for a refuge of such an expanse. Thus in territories where the adjacent areas are adequately populated a mutual supervision of the people by one another is very useful. But in a region so poorly populated as the south-western part of Mongolia the possibility of such control is simply excluded.

The solution planned in the Soviet Union seems to be much better. There they think of settling the wild horses on one of the islands of the Aral Sea. The saiga-antelopes, gazelles and kulans settled on that island earlier are already proliferating successfully and undisturbed. Since all three of these species live together with the Mongolian wild horse in free nature, it is quite certain that this habitat would suit the wild horse too.

In maintaining the Przevalsky horse, Mongolian wild horses living in free nature would play, first of all, the part of an étalon. At present this role is played by Orlitza III–Mongol, the only Mongolian wild horse that was born in free nature and lives in captivity. It is evident that wild horses kept in captivity for several generations undergo changes if compared with such as live in free nature. Therefore it is useful if there are individuals compared with which it can be stated to what extent changes are taking place, and what kind of transformations captive wild horses are subject to. But Orlitza III, who lives in Askania Nova, is twenty-three years of age, and will have to be replaced by a new horse sooner or later.

For this purpose individuals of Przevalsky horses living in free nature ought to be caught now and then. However, they should no longer be captured by shooting the mares or by long chases, but by using guns that shoot cartridges filled with tranquillizers. Such a gun (Cap-Chur-Gun) was successfully tried out on Przevalsky horses at Catskill Game Farm. At the same time the quantity of succinyl-chlorid that has an adequate effect on wild horses but is not yet poisonous was established. In the case of adult horses in a good condition this quantity is 170–180 mg and causes, within one minute to six, an incapacity to move, which lasts three to twelve minutes. This time is quite enough for tying up a foal and placing it on a vehicle—if this is done by practised personnel. However, to achieve this it would be necessary first of all for the number of Przevalsky horses to increase in a wildlife refuge area.

Two principal questions arise in connection with Przevalsky horses in captivity. One is that of inbreeding and the degeneration ensuing from it, and the other the problem of over-refinement. Experiences have shown that the former need not be dealt with so much, since the stud-book of Przevalsky horses contains the necessary data on all Mongolian wild horses in zoos (with the exception of some of the wild horses at Woburn). On the basis of these entries the breeders can contrive to avoid the inbreeding that may lead to degeneration.

But over-refinement is a phenomenon that has already appeared in the stock of wild horses in zoological gardens. The light mane and hairs of the tail, the white marks and the dark spots on the coat all indicate this. So do the changes the proportions of the body have undergone, which have produced less thickset individuals of "nobler" forms, closer to domestic horses. And as soon as the transformations in colour and in shape become more prominent we are confronted with phenomena of domestication.

Such are for instance increases of variations, shortening and broadening of the nose, diminution of the teeth, and along with this shortening of the length of the row of molars, widening of the brain skull, etc. The sexual rhythm, too, gets changed and is evident in the extension of birth over practically all the year. Side by side with this the sexual maturation of wild horses, which is a rather lengthy process, takes place much quicker in zoological gardens—owing to better feeding and protection.

What could be the cure for this over-refinement? Nothing but the creation of conditions of life closest to those in free nature, and strict control of breeding. Clearly no such conditions of life can be ensured for Mongolian wild horses in zoos—and not even in animal parks—as in their original habitat. Nobody can provide this—nor can anybody expect it. But by no means need wild horses in captivity be constrained within a small space surrounded by the bars or wire netting of an old fashioned zoo. Spacious paddocks must be provided for them, where they can move about to their heart's content. By no means must the soil of the paddock be humid; it must be dry and may be pebbly or, here and there, even stony.

In free paddocks wild horses can move more, but sometimes they do not by their own free will. For this reason Anghi suggested that they should be induced to move by the introduction of not-too-high obstacles, water ditches and steep ascents. Since the animals would jump over these only if motivated to do so, they should be built in front of watering and feeding places, thus forcing the horses to pass them if they want to get at their fodder and drink.

Anyhow, it would be useful to remove the wild horses from zoos and to settle them in nature conservation areas, provided these are not too damp. This would not be a final settlement for the different animals, only a temporary one. Freer space and movement there would have a good effect on the animals' physique and, clearly, on their psyche as well. When the animals have "recovered" in this way they can be brought back into the zoos.

On the other hand, it might not be expedient from this point to saddle and break to the rein wild horses in zoos while young. No doubt regular exercise would favourably affect the development of their bone structure; on the other hand, riding may bring about some changes in the shape of their bodies too. Besides, this would be domestication—a thing we should not inflict on them, for we should be happiest to keep them in their original wild state.

Foraging of wild horses kept in captivity should also be strictly controlled. It is to be borne in mind that in free nature they have no access to the kinds of compact fodder that we feed them on, and by providing too much we may disturb the rhythm of their development.

Finally, severe selection may also prove expedient: individuals showing major phenomena of over-refinement should be mercilessly excluded from breeding. As far as mating is concerned, individuals should be mated, first and foremost, which are close to the international étalon.

If the experiments aimed at ensuring the survival of the Mongolian wild horse are successful and the stock in zoological gardens and animal parks can be appropriately increased in numbers, and if the animals living in free nature can be saved from extinction, the time may soon come when individuals brought up in zoos might be settled in free nature. At present this may sound Utopian, but it may prove feasible in the future.

It is highly probable that some of the Mongolian wild horses kept in captivity for several generations would soon perish if resettled in the wild. These horses have been protected by man for a long time and have no doubt forgotten what it is to struggle for their lives. In fights with the stallions living in free nature those coming from captivity would certainly be vanquished, whereas the mares would be threatened by beasts of prey. In the beginning they might even have difficulties in finding food. But one point is clear: the survivors would soon get adjusted to their original habitat, and the Mongolian steppe would shortly correct the transformations wrought by long captivity on wild horses kept in zoos. And this would surely be a welcome change, which, if successfully realized, might be the right course for maintaining the Przevalsky horse.

# SELECTED BIBLIOGRAPHY

The following list contains not only the most important sources used in writing the present work but also such books as give the reader detailed information on the questions discussed here.

BANNIKOV, A. A. Distribution géographique et biologie du cheval sauvage et du chameau de Mongolie (Equus przewalskii et Camelus bactrianus). Mammalia 1 (1958) pp. 152–60.

BIBIKOVA, V. I. Kizutcheniyu drvneyshik domashnikh loshadey Vostotchnoy Evropy. (Studies on ancient domestic horses in East Europe). Byulleten Moskovskogo Obshtchestva Ospytateley Prirody, Otdel Biologitcheskiy. 3 (1967) pp. 106–18.

BÖKÖNYI, S. Data on Iron Age Horses of Central and Eastern Europe. Bulletin of American School of Prehistoric Research. 25. Cambridge (Mass.) 1968.

BÜCHNER, E. A. The Przewalski Horse in the Work of W. W. Salensky. (In Russian) Petersburg 1903.

CAMP, C. L. and SMITH, N. Phylogeny and function of the digital ligaments of the horse. Memoirs of the University of California. 13 (1942) pp. 69–124.

EQUUS. Proceedings of the Ist International Symposium on Przewalski Horse, organised by the Zoological Garden in Prague, September 5th–September 8th 1959. Prague 1961.

EQUUS. Proceedings of the IInd International Symposium on Przewalski Horse organised by the Tierpark Berlin, January 18th–January 20th 1965. Berlin 1967.

FALZ-FEIN, W. Askania Nova, Neudamm 1930.

GARRUTT, E. W., SOKOLOV, I. I. and SALESSKAYA, T. N. Erforschung und Zucht des Przewalski-Pferdes (Equus przewalskii

Poljakoff) in der Sowjetunion. Zeitschrift fur Tierzüchtung und Züchtungsbiologie. 82, 4 (1966) pp. 377-426.

GROMOVA, V. History of Horses (Equus genus) in Early Times. I–II (In Russian) Trudy Poleontoloitcheskogo Instituta. XVII. Moscow–Leningrad, 1949.

GROMOVA, V. On the skeleton of the tarpan (Equus caballus gmelini Ant.) and of other present day wild horses. (In Russian) Byulleten Moskovskogo Obshtchestva Ospytateley Prirody, Otdel Biologii. LXIV, 4, (1959) pp. 99-124.

HAGENBECK, C. Von Tieren und Menschen. Leipzig 1928.

HECK, H. Bemarkungen über die Mähne der Urwildpferde. Das Tier und wir. 1936. pp. 1-14.

HEPTNER, W. G. Notes on the tarpans. (In Russian) Zoologicseszkij Zsurnal. 34 (1955) pp. 1404-23.

KASZAB, Z. Recent occurrence of the Przewalski horse (Equus przewalskii Poljakoff) in Mongolia. (In Hungarian) Allattani Közlemenyek. LIV (1967) pp. 63-5.

LIGETI, L. (Transl.) A mongolok titkos története (Monga-un Niuca tobcaan)(The Secret History of the Mongols) Budapest, 1962.

LUNDHOLM, B. Abstammung und Domestikation des Hauspferdes. Zoologiska Bidrag fram Uppsala. 27. Uppsala 1947.

MOHR, E. Das Urwildpferd. Die Neue Brehm-Bücherei. 249. Wittenberg-Lutherstadt. 1959.

MOHR, E. The Asiatic wild horse. London (Allen Co.) 1971.

NOBIS, G. Vom Wildpferd zum Hauspferd. Fundamenta. Ser.B, Vol. 6. Köln (Böhlau Verlag) 1971.

PFIZENMAYER, E. W. Mammutleichen und Urwaldmenschen in Nordost-Sibirien. Leipzig 1926.

POLJAKOW, I. S. Supposed new species of horse from Central Asia. Ann. Mag. Nat-Hist. 5 (1881) pp. 16-26.

PRZEWALSKI, N. M. From Saissan through Chami to the upper reaches of Hoang-ho. (In Russian) St. Petersburg 1883.

SALENSKY, W. W. Prjewalsky's Horse. (With an introduction by J. C. Ewart) London 1907.

SIMPSON, G. G. Horses. New York 1961.

VITT, W. O. The horses of the kurgans of Pazyryk. (In Russian) Sovietskaya Archeologiya XVI (1952) pp. 11-56.

VOLF, J. General Pedigree Book of the Przewalski Horse. Prague 1970.

# INDEX

WATFORD CENTRAL